CAREERS in

SOCIAL & REHABILITATION SERVICES

CAREERS in

SOCIAL & REHABILITATION SERVICES

GERALDINE GARNER

THIRD EDITION

New York Chicago San Francisco Lisbon London Madrid Mexico City
Milan New Delhi San Juan Seoul Singapore Sydney Toronto

The McGraw-Hill Companies

Library of Congress Cataloging-in-Publication Data

Garner, Geraldine O.
    Careers in social and rehabilitation services / by Geraldine O. Garner.—3rd ed.
      p.   cm.
    ISBN 0-07-149313-1 (alk. paper)
     1. Social service—Vocational guidance—United States.   2. Rehabilitation—
Vocational guidance—United States.   3. Hospitals—Rehabilitation services—Vocational
guidance—United States.   I. Title.

   HV10.5.G39 2008
   361.973023—dc22
                                       2007047010

1 2 3 4 5 6 7 8 9 0 DOC/DOC 0 9 8

ISBN 978-0-07-149313-0
MHID   0-07-149313-1

McGraw-Hill books are available at special quantity discounts to use as premiums and sales
promotions or for use in corporate training programs. To contact a representative, please visit
the Contact Us pages at www.mhprofessional.com.

This book is printed on acid-free paper.

This book is dedicated to my mother and father. As a child, they showed me what it means to be a loving caregiver.

CONTENTS

ACKNOWLEDGMENTS

In the beginning, the goal of this book was to help undergraduate students in rehabilitation counseling understand the wide range of career opportunities that they could pursue. With each edition of the book it has become increasingly clear that the fields of social and rehabilitation services are dynamic and are changing at a rapid pace. When so many in our country and around the world need the special skills, expertise, and personal characteristics of social workers and rehabilitation professionals, it is now the goal of this book to introduce even more people to the rewarding opportunities that await people who study and train for this field.

The contributors to this third edition clearly demonstrate how challenging and satisfying careers in social and rehabilitation services can be. Ann McLaughlin, M.S.W., Director, NGOabroad, has written a new chapter on the international experiences that are possible for people educated and prepared as social workers and rehabilitation specialists. Her insights into how to prepare yourself and become educated for such opportunities are invaluable.

In this edition, the chapter on therapeutic services has been expanded and updated thanks to the contributions of many dedicated professionals. They include

Diane U. Jette, PT, D.Sc., of the University of Vermont
Shelly J. Lane, Ph.D., OTR/L, FAOTA, of Virginia Commonwealth
   University

Dr. Jessica Young, LCPC, ADTR, GLCMA, of the Illinois Chapter of the American Dance Therapy Association and Columbia College Chicago

Nancy Easterling, M.S.W., HTM, of the American Horticultural Therapist Association and the North Carolina Botanical Garden at the University of North Carolina at Chapel Hill

Gaye Horton of the American Horticultural Therapist Association

Judy Simpson, MHP, MT-BC, of the American Music Therapy Association

Marie E. Jetté, SLP-CCC, of the Center for Laryngeal Surgery and Voice Rehabilitation at Massachusetts General Hospital.

I want to thank each of these talented writers for their contributions to this book. Without them, it would not be possible to bring you the most up-to-date information about careers in the therapeutic areas of social and rehabilitation services.

CHAPTER

1

REHABILITATION SERVICES

Technology touches all aspects of our life today. We can now take and send pictures and videos with our phones. We can also post those pictures and videos on the Web through social networks, and they instantly become accessible all over the world. We can talk to each other instantly with IM technology. High-tech medical advances can take pictures deep within our bodies, making diagnoses easier and, in some cases, avoiding exploratory surgeries.

High-tech advances are all around us. They make everyday life easier and can improve the quality of life for people with disabilities. These advances are changing our lives in many ways. As a result, one might think that the only career opportunities of the future are those of computer scientist, programmer, or engineer. That is definitely not the case. As technical advances change the way we live, the work we do, and the health care we receive, human needs and conditions also change. These changes are requiring more workers at all levels of the social services and medical fields. Professionals in the fields of social and rehabilitation services play critical roles in these fields and have a wide range of responsibilities, including the following:

- Assisting and advocating for patient access to quality services within the health-care industry
- Providing disaster relief and grief counseling to people and communities that suffer major loss

- Helping people with physical, mental, or emotional disabilities to improve their quality of life
- Working with people with substance abuse problems and other addictions
- Working with adult and/or juvenile public offenders
- Working with students in elementary, middle, and high schools as well as colleges and universities
- Serving clients and their families who rely on local, state, and federal government agencies or in military-related organizations
- Collaborating with community organizations and the community at large to attain a higher quality of life for the citizens of the area
- Improving cultural, ethnic, and racial empathy to advance and sustain individual and community growth and development
- Assisting in the promotion of spiritual, ethical, religious, and other human values essential to full development
- Helping to develop healthy family systems
- Counseling in employment and/or career development settings

The professionals in rehabilitation services are those on the front lines of these and other social issues of our time. As a result, careers in the diverse field of rehabilitation services are among the most competitive of all professions.

While helping others is the hallmark of this career field, it is not enough simply to like people. It is important to really enjoy working with people and to gain and maintain the knowledge and expertise to do so effectively. Working with people can be exciting and rewarding. It can also be highly stressful and demanding. Therefore, rehabilitation services professionals and social workers must have objectivity, patience, maturity, and appropriate training, supervision, and experience.

THE HISTORY OF REHABILITATION SERVICES

Although social consciousness and concern for others have been part of humanity from the beginning of time, it is widely considered that the 1889 founding of Hull House in Chicago was the birth of the field we now call social work in the United States. Hull House represented Jane Addams's philosophy of helping others gain a better standard of living. That philosophy continues today.

After World War I, fields such as social work, occupational therapy, and rehabilitation counseling began to be viewed as true occupations. The turning point was the passage of legislation directed at assisting veterans returning from the war. The legislation of the 1920s forged a relationship between the federal and state governments to provide rehabilitation programs. These programs were initially limited to job retraining and training of veterans. Over time the scope and influence of rehabilitation services professionals and programs have increased.

During the 1930s the social consequences of the Great Depression became the impetus for federal, state, and local governments to work with the private sector to meet the overall needs of all people, not just veterans. But again the emphasis was on jobs.

Subsequent federal legislation in the area of rehabilitation allowed for corrective surgery, therapeutic treatment, and hospitalization. This legislation greatly expanded opportunities in the field and made training and counseling more effective.

The range of professional opportunities in the field of rehabilitation services greatly expanded when legislation was passed to provide money to train doctors, nurses, rehabilitation counselors, physical therapists, occupational therapists, social workers, and other rehabilitation professionals. The passage of the Americans with Disabilities Act in 1990 had the same impact on the field.

In 1996, President Clinton signed the Personal Responsibility and Work Opportunity Reconciliation Act. This law changed welfare programs in the United States from income maintenance programs to employment programs. Its original goal was to help welfare recipients qualify for government jobs. In addition, President Clinton urged private-sector businesses, nonprofit organizations, and religious groups to train and employ welfare recipients. This legislation changed the demand for professionals working with the most financially disadvantaged in our society. It has required the development of new skills in preparing, placing, and supporting clients in the search for employment opportunities, with the goal of lifting these clients out of poverty.

REHABILITATION SERVICES TODAY

A new age and attitude in rehabilitation services is upon us. It offers many diverse career opportunities. Each occupation provides a high degree of responsibility and challenge in caring for the special needs of patients and clients. Typically the people served by social and rehabilitation professionals have personal, social, vocational, physical, educational, and/or spiritual challenges.

TYPES OF WORK PERFORMED

Rehabilitation services professionals perform a range of duties. The types of responsibilities they perform tend to fall into four categories.

Client Support Responsibilities
Conducting intake
Facilitating logistics and transportation
Motivating clients to continue with their treatment programs
Working with families and significant others
Performing client evaluation and follow-up

Treatment Responsibilities
Performing crisis intervention
Participating in the development of treatment plans
Coordinating the implementation of the treatment plan
Identifying treatment gaps and overlaps
Conducting individual and group counseling sessions
Providing consultation on special cases

Outreach Responsibilities
Performing community outreach
Identifying, mobilizing, and coordinating community resources
Seeking and using support networks
Referring clients to other professionals and/or services
Providing education and prevention strategies

Administrative Responsibilities
Reporting and record keeping
Assisting in program development
Training other staff
Providing program consultation

Because the responsibilities of rehabilitation services professionals are closely tied to the health and well-being of other human beings, the levels of authority vary greatly depending on the amount of education and the years of experience one possesses.

At the entry level, people who have the title of aides perform basic tasks such as personal care and feeding of patients or transportation of clients. Their work frees professionals and medical staff to concentrate on treatment and therapies. While aides tend to have high school diplomas, it is generally not required. Consequently, sometimes aides are volunteers who want to see what the field is all about. Some aides are workers who have a real interest in the occupational area but, for various reasons, have not completed the levels of education required for other positions in the field.

Assistants perform support tasks such as patient/client intake and follow-up, treatment setup, and patient assistance. These individuals may or may not have a college degree, but they usually have completed some form of specialized training. This may be on-the-job training, technical school training, or completion of a junior or community college program. In some cases, the preparation may actually be a specialized bachelor's degree program.

Counselors and social workers perform tasks such as facilitating individual and group counseling sessions, administering and interpreting aptitude and interest tests, and making referrals to other professionals. Counselors and social workers generally hold master's degrees. Some hold doctorates. It should be noted that some people might have a bachelor of social work (B.S.W.) or bachelor of rehabilitation services. In these instances, the level of responsibility is greatly limited when compared to those with a master's degree. Counselors and social workers may also be certified by an appropriate professional agency and licensed by the state in which they work.

Therapists generally have completed a related bachelor's and master's degree and additional clinical experience. Some can hold doctorates. They perform specialized treatments designed to rehabilitate patients physically and/or psychologically. Therapists are almost always certified by an appropriate professional group. Some can also be licensed.

Physicians perform medical treatments. The treatments can range from clinical diagnosis to surgery. These professionals have not only completed undergraduate and medical school, they have also completed internships and residency programs in their areas of specialization. All physicians are licensed to practice medicine and can be board certified in a clinical area.

WORK SETTINGS

People in rehabilitation services work in a variety of settings. A partial list of the work settings for rehabilitation services professionals includes hospitals; rehabilitation centers; mental health clinics; guidance centers; nonprofit services agencies; federal, state, county, and municipal government agencies; halfway houses and group homes; public and private schools, colleges, and universities; churches and synagogues; correctional institutions and courts; and business and industry. Some are self-employed as licensed practitioners. The employment options are almost limitless.

CHARACTERISTICS OF PEOPLE IN REHABILITATION SERVICES

It is important for those who work in rehabilitation services to care about the needs and welfare of people. While professionals in this area are often characterized as being patient, sincere, and interested in helping others, they also have to be tough-minded in a constructive manner and be interested in effecting positive change. This is not always easy.

Professionals in rehabilitation services should be able to gain the trust of others easily and to think logically. They must communicate well with people, particularly people under a great deal of stress. Their written and oral communication skills should be excellent. Rehabilitation services professionals often have to motivate their clients as well as influence people who can assist and support their clients.

PREPARING FOR A CAREER IN REHABILITATION SERVICES

Education is critical to preparing for and advancing in a rehabilitation services career field. From rehabilitation assistants to psychiatrists, Ph.D. rehabilitation counselors, and social workers, all need a good foundation in math, science, social sciences, and human development. While it is not necessary for rehabilitation services professionals to know how to build and program high-tech devices, it is necessary for them to know how to use them effectively for their patients and clients.

During High School

During high school, it is advisable to take courses in English, a foreign language, mathematics, social science, physical education, and the sciences. In addition to these courses, it is highly recommended that future professionals take elective courses in such areas as government, media, minority studies/literature, psychology, sociology, and anatomy.

High school students who are interested in careers in rehabilitation services should become actively involved in social service clubs and volunteer in their community. Team sports, student government leadership roles, and part-time jobs in social service–related organizations are also highly recommended. The more a high school student works with different populations and in different settings, the easier it will be to focus future studies and experiences and develop a sufficient level of expertise to make a significant contribution to his or her chosen field.

During College

Many people major in rehabilitation services, social work, sociology, or psychology to prepare for a career in social and rehabilitation services. Those planning to enter the field as physicians will need a college curriculum that includes a sufficient number of physical or life sciences courses to gain entry to medical school.

A variety of majors are good preparation for careers in social and rehabilitation services. The liberal arts, the life and physical sciences, the arts, the social sciences, premedicine, engineering, and agriculture all provide an excellent foundation for a career in rehabilitation services.

As in high school, it is extremely important to continue to gain as much related experience as possible. Campus volunteer programs, summer and part-time jobs, academic internships, and cooperative education all provide excellent opportunities to build on the academic foundation of college.

Remember that advancement in this field requires not only higher levels of education but also relevant experience. Therefore, it is advisable to seek a variety of experiences during your undergraduate program. These experiences help you clarify your career focus for employment or graduate/professional school.

In some rehabilitation services fields, a graduate degree or medical degree is the minimum education requirement for entry into the field. This is particularly true in many medical fields.

LICENSURE AND CERTIFICATION

There are numerous professions within the rehabilitation field that require licensure or certification. The purpose of licensure or certification is to ensure that all members of the profession meet minimum educational and experience requirements and are competent to practice. In healthcare situations, practicing without a required license is usually a serious crime.

Each state establishes its own licensure requirements. Likewise, in Canada, each province establishes its own licensing requirements. Whether in the United States or in Canada, professional licenses are usually valid only within the state or province in which it is granted.

There can be significant variations among states or provinces regarding the qualifications for each type of licensing, whether it is for rehabilitation counselors, social workers, mental health nurses, or psychologists. However, there can be cases where one state or province will accept a license issued by another state or province. This situation, known as reciprocity, permits the professional to move to another state or province to work without having to take that state's licensure examination.

Some professions require more than one license. In these situations, the additional license or certification is required for a specialty in the particular profession.

OUTLOOK AND EARNINGS

According to recent commercial and government publications, rehabilitation services occupations are expected to grow faster than average. Predictions gauge that growth will be particularly strong in care for the aging, the homeless, and the mentally impaired and developmentally disabled.

The growing elderly population will need more adult day care. New methods of treating the mentally and physically disabled will require more group homes and residential-care facilities. Likewise, the number of community-based programs and group residences for the homeless are expected to increase.

Historically, rehabilitation services professions have not typically paid high salaries. However, substantial salary increases have been reported for graduates majoring in liberal arts areas in recent years. For many jobs in the area of social and rehabilitation services, a liberal arts degree is required for entry-level positions in the rehabilitation services field. It is important to know that government funding of many social service programs often determines what will be paid to providers. Therefore, salaries in the rehabilitation field reflect federal, state, and local budgets. That means that when these budgets are strong, job opportunities and salaries will be stronger. When government budgets are tight, positions can be cut and salaries can decrease for entry-level positions and remain flat for experienced workers.

While salaries will depend on your specific rehabilitation specialty, where you decide to work, and current budget situations, national salary figures are available from the U.S. Bureau of Labor Statistics (http://stats.bls.gov). These figures are compiled from census data and can be somewhat dated at the time of publication. For example, in 2007, the Bureau of Labor Statistics was reporting median salaries for vocational rehabilitation counselors based on 2004 data. The median salary was reported to be $27,800, which means that half of the vocational rehabilitation counselors included in the data made more than that and the other half made less.

Internet resources tend to be more up-to-date and can help you learn what current salary rates are for entry-level to experienced professionals in the specific area where you plan to work. For people working in the United States, Salary Wizard (http://swz.salary.com) is a good website for researching current salary rates. In 2007, Salary Wizard reported the median salary for vocational rehabilitation counselors to be $50,467. This means that half of all vocational rehabilitation counselors in this study made less and half made more than this amount. In addition to being more current, the Salary Wizard allows you to search salary data by state for improved accuracy.

Generally speaking, high levels of compensation are not associated with most of the occupations in this area. Therefore, it is important not to set earnings expectations too high.

There are areas of rehabilitation services that command higher-than-average salaries. Psychiatry is a good example. However, it is important to note that the areas of rehabilitation services that command higher salaries also require higher levels of education, years of supervised clinical experience, and licensure or certification.

ABOUT THIS BOOK

This book contains an overview of the profession plus chapters on specific occupations within the field of social and rehabilitation services. Each occupational field is discussed in terms of the work performed, the types of people served, the variety of work settings, the training and qualifications required, and advancement possibilities.

The book also discusses why it is so important that prospective social and rehabilitation services professionals begin to identify the populations and settings in which they are most interested in working. To help in this process this book will address the different types of people that can be served, the different levels of education necessary for entry into specific occupations, and the wide variety of settings in which to work. These distinctions are very important to career satisfaction and success.

Finally, the book includes many resources in the appendixes. Appendixes A and B cover professional organizations in the United States and Canada. Appendix C lists other websites of interest. And Appendixes D and E are lists of colleges and universities offering programs in social and rehabilitation services in the United States and Canada.

CHAPTER

2

SO YOU'RE GOOD WITH PEOPLE

One of the chief characteristics of people in the field of social and reha-bilitation services is that they are good with people. When rehabilitation professionals are asked why they decided to go into rehabilitation services, they will almost always give this reason.

Being good with people is important; however, it's a characteristic that you need to examine more closely. It is important to know what being good with people means to you. That is the only way to find the right fit with a career in the wide field of social and rehabilitation services.

THE TYPES OF PEOPLE YOU WOULD SERVE BEST

There are many types of people who need the services of social and rehabil-itation professionals. But every rehabilitation services professional cannot be trained in or interested in working with all of these people. Likewise, there are many types of problems that people have to face, and no rehabili-tation services professional is qualified to handle all of them.

When considering a career in social work or rehabilitation services, it is important to consider with what type of people you are most interested in working and what type of problems you are most interested in addressing. Do you like to work with the elderly? Are you interested in working with children who have developmental disabilities? What about athletes with sports related injuries?

Keep in mind that no one is good with all people. And that's OK, because it is important to select a population that will provide you with the most personal fulfillment. That is an important part of your career decision making.

It is crucial to think about the types of people who need the services of a rehabilitation professional. In preparing for the field of social and rehabilitation services, you will want to pursue the type of education that focuses on the group or groups with whom you would most like to work. This is a necessary first step in the preparation process because social and rehabilitation services professionals need to become increasingly more knowledgeable about the psychological, sociological, and physiological needs of the population they intend to serve.

The following is a collection of comparative questions to start the thinking process.

- Am I more interested in working with babies than with schoolchildren?

    Yes   No   Neither

- Am I more interested in working with small children than with teenagers?

    Yes   No   Neither

- Am I more interested in working with teenagers than with college students?

    Yes   No   Neither

- Am I more interested in working with adults than with children?

    Yes   No   Neither

- Am I more interested in working with the elderly than with children or adults?

    Yes   No   Neither

- Am I more interested in working with girls than with boys?

    Yes   No   Neither

- Am I more interested in working with women than with men?

    Yes   No   Neither

- Am I more interested in working with a particular ethnic group or nationality?

    Yes   No

- Am I more interested in working with a certain religious group?

    Yes   No

Likewise, career satisfaction is closely related to higher levels of knowledge about issues that a professional addresses. Therefore, it is important to consider the types of physical and mental challenges that interest you, as well as whom you would like to help. The range of human issues is extensive, and you might feel that you want to address them all. Your educational preparation will provide a broad overview of human issues and conditions. But throughout the educational process, you will want to begin to narrow your areas of interest in order to focus your knowledge and expertise.

The following is a partial list of issues that social and rehabilitation services professionals address. The columns indicate a high level of interest (HI), moderate level of interest (MI), low level of interest (LI), or no interest (NI).

Homelessness or inadequate housing	HI	MI	LI	NI
Unemployment	HI	MI	LI	NI
Lack of job skills	HI	MI	LI	NI
Financial mismanagement	HI	MI	LI	NI
Illness	HI	MI	LI	NI
Physical disability	HI	MI	LI	NI
Mental disability	HI	MI	LI	NI
Unwanted pregnancy	HI	MI	LI	NI
Teenage pregnancy	HI	MI	LI	NI
Alcohol abuse	HI	MI	LI	NI
Drug abuse	HI	MI	LI	NI
Antisocial behavior	HI	MI	LI	NI
Child abuse	HI	MI	LI	NI
Spouse abuse	HI	MI	LI	NI
Divorce	HI	MI	LI	NI
Family conflict	HI	MI	LI	NI
Criminal insanity	HI	MI	LI	NI
Grief counseling	HI	MI	LI	NI
First responders and disaster relief	HI	MI	LI	NI

WORK SETTINGS THAT PERMIT YOU TO SUCCEED

Social and rehabilitation services occupations provide a range of opportunities for people to pursue careers in settings that complement their interests and knowledge. These professionals are found in such diverse institutions as the following:

- Schools, colleges, and universities
- Hospitals
- Rehab centers
- Correctional institutions
- Business and industry
- Social service agencies—both public and private
- Faith-based organizations, including churches
- Public welfare offices
- Child welfare organizations
- Nursing homes
- Group homes
- Halfway houses
- Consulting services
- Private medical practices
- Private counseling practices
- Government agencies

Those interested in working in the field of social and rehabilitation services should begin to identify the settings where they have the most interest and where they have, or are willing to develop, the expertise necessary to serve the specific population.

Using the list on this page and the additional information from the work settings section in each chapter, you can begin to identify either the areas of interest or areas that can be crossed off the list because of a lack of interest. By so doing, it is possible to narrow your focus and concentrate efforts in preparing for and succeeding in a professional area that meets your personal needs, interests, and abilities. This is important in the field of social and rehabilitation services because success means a positive impact on the quality of life of the people you serve.

THE SKILLS YOU WILL NEED

To help you decide if you have the personal skills and abilities necessary for a career in social and rehabilitation services, you can use a free online service called O*NET at http://online.onetcenter.org. It is a good source of occupational information and is continually updated to assure that you have access to current data about careers in which you are interested. In addition to the lists of skills and abilities needed in social and rehabilitation services, the database also provides helpful career exploration tools.

According to O*NET, social and rehabilitation services professionals have good skills and abilities in the following areas. And O*NET notes that reasonable accommodations may be made for some of these skills and abilities in order to enable people with disabilities to achieve them. For example, a deaf counselor can actively "listen" through the use of sign language; a person who is blind may use assistive technology to "see" written details.

See the following lists to determine what skills and abilities you bring to the table.

Skills

- **Active listening.** Giving full attention to what other people are saying, taking time to understand the points being made, asking questions as appropriate and not interrupting at inappropriate times.
- **Social perceptiveness.** Being aware of others' reactions and understanding why they react as they do.
- **Critical thinking.** Using logic and reasoning to identify the strengths and weaknesses of alternative solutions, conclusions, or approaches to problems.
- **Service orientation.** Actively looking for ways to help people.
- **Active learning.** Understanding the implications of new information for both current and future problem solving and decision making.
- **Learning strategies.** Selecting and using training/instructional methods and procedures appropriate for the situation when learning or teaching new things.
- **Speaking.** Talking to others to convey information effectively.
- **Time management.** Managing one's own time and the time of others.
- **Reading comprehension.** Understanding written sentences and paragraphs in work-related documents.
- **Monitoring.** Monitoring/assessing the performance of yourself, other individuals, or organizations to make improvements or take corrective action.

Abilities

- **Oral expression.** The ability to communicate information and ideas in speaking so others will understand.
- **Oral comprehension.** The ability to listen to and understand information and ideas presented through spoken words and sentences.
- **Problem sensitivity.** The ability to tell when something is wrong or is likely to go wrong; it does not involve solving the problem, only recognizing there is a problem.
- **Speech clarity.** The ability to speak clearly so others can understand you.
- **Inductive reasoning.** The ability to combine pieces of information to form general rules or conclusions (includes finding a relationship among seemingly unrelated events).
- **Deductive reasoning.** The ability to apply general rules to specific problems to produce answers that make sense.
- **Speech recognition.** The ability to identify and understand the speech of another person.
- **Written comprehension.** The ability to read and understand information and ideas presented in writing.
- **Written expression.** The ability to communicate information and ideas in writing so others will understand.
- **Near vision.** The ability to see details at close range (within a few feet of the observer).

HOW TO PAY FOR YOUR EDUCATION

As in so many fields, there is a strong relationship between education and advancement. The more education a social and rehabilitation services professional has, the more opportunities for advancement there will be. However, unlike some professions, there are opportunities for people without high school diplomas as well as for those with advanced and professional degrees in areas such as medicine and law.

The field provides great flexibility for movement, growth, and challenge. Therefore, it is important to think about personal goals and finances when considering the level of education you will need to complete to pursue the career that best fits you. To assist in this planning, each chapter in this book provides information on the level of education needed to enter and advance in each area. The requirements and demands of each field must be balanced against the personal values, abilities, needs, and resources of each prospective professional.

Paying for your education can be a concern. However, you might qualify for scholarships or grants, which don't have to be repaid, or federal, state, or university student loans, which do have to be repaid.

It is important to note that there are loan forgiveness programs, depending on the field of study that you have chosen in the fields of social and rehabilitation services. The National Association for Social Work (NASW) provides an excellent website that provides detailed information about these programs (socialworkers.org/advocacy/issues/loanforgiveness.asp). It is important to note that not all social and rehabilitation services career areas are covered by loan forgiveness programs at the federal and state level. However, it's worth checking various websites, because the information can change yearly. Check the websites regularly and talk to your college or university financial aid office about the options that are available to you.

The following is a list of programs and offices that could be helpful to you:

American Programs

Perkins Loan Forgiveness Program
staffordloan.com/repayment/federal-student-loan-forgiveness.php
finaid.org/loans/forgiveness.phtml

National Health Service Corp—Federal Program
http://nhsc.bhpr.hrsa.gov/join_us/lrp.cfm

National Institutes of Health (NIH)—Loan Forgiveness for Researchers
lrp.nih.gov

National Association of Social Workers
socialworkers.org/advocacy/issues/loanforgiveness.asp

If you are meeting the health-care needs of underserved communities in your state, you might qualify for a loan forgiveness program. However, all states do not offer these programs for every social and rehabilitation services career field. To gain accurate and up-to-date information, it is highly recommended that you check appropriate state websites to determine if there are programs for which you might qualify. Some of those websites include the following:

HRSA Bureau of Health Professions: Geriatrics, Health Education, Rural Health, Allied Health, Chiropractic
http://bhpr.hrsa.gov/interdisciplinary

National Health Service Corp—State Loan Repayment Program
http://nhsc.bhpr.hrsa.gov/join_us/slrp.cfm

National Association of Social Workers
socialworkers.org/advocacy/issues/loanForgiveness.asp
  (See "Updates and Letters" on this site.)

Canadian Programs

Compared to the financial aid in the United States, many Canadian citizens are eligible for substantially lower tuition rates at colleges and universities. Nonetheless, you might still need assistance with tuition costs. Each Canadian province maintains its own support organizations and financial aid opportunities for citizens and permanent residents. Information on financial aid resources in your home province is available at worldwide learn.com/financial-aid/canadian-students.htm and the following specific province websites:

Alberta: alis.gov.ab.ca/studentsfinance/main.asp
British Columbia: aved.gov.bc.ca/studentaidbc/welcome.htm
Manitoba: gov.mb.ca/educate/sfa/pages/sfafrontdoor_en.html
New Brunswick: studentaid.gnb.ca
Newfoundland and Labrador: worldwidelearn.com/financial-aid/
    canadian-students.htm
Northwest Territory: nwtsfa.gov.nt.ca

Nunavut: nac.nu.ca/student/fans.htm

Nova Scotia: http://studentloans.ednet.ns.ca

Ontario: http://osap.gov.on.ca

Prince Edward Island: gov.pe.ca/educ

Quebec: afe.gov.qc.ca

Saskatchewan: sasked.gov.sk.ca/branches/sfa/student_loans

Yukon: worldwidelearn/com/financial-aid/canadian-students.htm

CHAPTER

3

REHABILITATION COUNSELING

According to the U.S. Department of Labor, there are over 500,000 counselors in the United States. They are classified in the following counseling specialties:

Educational, vocational, and school counselors	248,000
Rehabilitation counselors	131,000
Mental health counselors	96,000
Substance abuse and behavioral disorder counselors	76,000
Marriage and family therapists	24,000

These counselors play an important role in the lives of the people they serve. By working diligently to improve the quality of life for their clients, rehabilitation counselors provide support, training, and opportunities.

According to the Bureau of Labor Statistics, the demand for rehabilitation professionals is expected to grow rapidly as societal conditions change. These conditions include homelessness, teenage pregnancies, the family stress of long-term unemployment, returning veterans, and an aging population. Likewise, advances in medical technology are resulting in more lives being saved. The recovery process from serious illnesses and injury requires rehabilitation counselors to work with physicians and therapists to help patients adjust and adapt to the changes that can occur in their lives.

In addition, as the population ages, there will also be a new demand to assure the quality of life that the elderly expect despite diminished capacity. These and other societal changes are expected to increase the demand for rehabilitation counselors in the years ahead.

THE WORK OF REHABILITATION COUNSELORS

The duties of a rehabilitation counselor vary depending on the population with whom the counselor works and the setting in which the work takes place. Regardless of the population or setting, rehabilitation counselors help people address the personal, social, physical, and vocational impact of their disabilities. They do this by using a combination of techniques such as the following:

- Vocational assessment
- Individual, group, and family counseling
- Medical services coordination
- Employment services and coordination
- Teaching leisure activities for health and well-being
- Developing and implementing rehabilitation plans
- Transferable skills assessment
- Job and task analysis
- Job-seeking skills training
- Labor market surveys
- Job development
- Job placement

By interviewing their clients (and sometimes their families) and by studying medical records and life histories, rehabilitation counselors arrange a program of medical care, vocational training, and/or job placement that meets the clients' needs. They may develop these programs alone or in consultation with other members of a treatment team.

Some rehabilitation counselors specialize in providing personal and vocational counseling for certain types of individuals and/or groups. Others work with a medical team to develop and implement a plan of recovery for patients who have suffered an injury or illness. Still other rehabilitation counselors work with clients to increase their capacity to live and work independently.

In general, rehabilitation counselors evaluate the overall strengths and limitations of their clients to help them find new avenues for meeting their needs, interests, and capabilities. Experienced rehabilitation counselors can become involved in developing and implementing agency programs to address the ongoing and changing needs of their special clients. Examples of this may be the introduction of job training and job-seeking skills for recovering addicts; programs in stress and financial management for the unemployed; and educational programs about community resources for residents of independent living centers.

The populations with whom rehabilitation counselors work vary greatly. Most rehabilitation counselors work only with groups about whom they have in-depth knowledge of abilities, needs, and interests. Some of these special groups include the blind, the mentally ill, the physically disabled, the developmentally disabled, the hearing impaired, the mentally retarded, battered women, autistic children, substance abusers, the elderly, and prisoners.

The clients of a rehabilitation counselor can be of any age, gender, ethnicity, or religion. Again, some counselors specialize within a larger group. For example, a rehabilitation counselor can work exclusively in the area of vocational rehabilitation and only work with veterans of war.

Some rehabilitation counselors serve not only their clients but also the families of their clients. Often rehabilitation counselors work with other social service professionals, medical specialists, therapists, and prospective employers. The opportunity to interact with people can be very broad in this occupation.

WHERE REHABILITATION COUNSELORS WORK

Most rehabilitation counselors work for public agencies such as rehab centers, sheltered workshops, nonprofit service agencies, hospitals, special schools, and training institutions. Some work in business and industry, particularly as part of a human resources team. Some work for insurance companies.

Increasingly, rehabilitation counselors are required to become certified or licensed. Licensure allows them to start a private practice, where they work for themselves, or to join a small group with a specialized practice.

HOW TO QUALIFY AS A REHABILITATION COUNSELOR

People who hold associate or bachelor's degrees in social services or rehabilitation services can qualify for entry-level positions such as intake specialists and activities coordinators in rehabilitation settings. However, increasingly, employers require a master's degree in rehabilitation counseling, counseling and guidance, or counseling psychology to provide direct patient and client services.

Typically, graduate programs in rehabilitation counseling require course work in five major areas, in addition to an internship. An internship is a supervised work experience in a setting that is closely related to your career goals. Most programs require students to work six hundred hours or more in this setting, where faculty and a qualified counselor in the agency or organization provide supervision. The five course work areas are as follows:

- **Foundations of rehabilitation.** Includes principles of rehabilitation; rehabilitation counseling ethics; the history, philosophy, and legislation of rehabilitation; and disabling conditions.
- **Client assessment.** Includes client information; principles, types, and techniques of assessments; the interpretation of assessment results; and resources for assessment.
- **Planning and service delivery.** Includes the synthesis of client information, rehabilitation plan development, service delivery systems, community resources, and case management.
- **Counseling and interviewing.** Includes theories and techniques in vocational and affective counseling, foundations of interviewing, principles of human behavior, and behavior change modalities.
- **Job development and placement.** Includes occupational and labor market information, job development, job-seeking skills training, placement, and follow-up.

Specific course titles might include the following:

Introduction to Rehabilitation
Medical Aspects of Rehabilitation
Psychological Aspects of Disability
Counseling Theories and Techniques
Counseling Theories and Techniques II
Group Counseling Techniques
Theory and Practice of Human Appraisal
Career Development and Job Placement
Rehabilitation Client Services
Practicum
Research Seminar
Internship

There are still some employers who will hire people who have only a bachelor's degree in an area such as rehabilitation services or other related fields. In these instances, the responsibilities of the position will probably be limited to the support responsibilities, as described in Chapter 1.

Employers also might require that rehabilitation counselors be certified by the Commission on Rehabilitation Counselor Certification. Completion of the graduate courses outlined previously tend to be adequate preparation for the certification exam. However, it is highly recommended that the commission be contacted for more in-depth information about the certification process, particularly in specialty areas (crccertification.com).

For those who wish to enter private practice, it will probably be necessary to meet the licensing requirements of the state in which practice is planned. Again, it is advisable to contact the appropriate state board of professional licensing to determine the course requirements and the level and amount of experience needed to take the written and/or oral licensing exam. In some states it is necessary to gain additional supervised experience after passing the written examination before full licensure is granted.

WHAT CAN YOU EARN AS A REHABILITATION COUNSELOR?

Salaries vary widely in the rehabilitation field, depending on the level of education you complete, the years of experience that you have, where you decide to work, and often the availability of government funding for these services. In 2007, those who held associate degrees, bachelor's degrees, or special certification had median salaries ranging from $22,800 to $39,000, depending on their level of education and the setting in which they worked.

For people who have a master's degree in rehabilitation counseling, psychology, or a related area of counseling, the median salary can be in the range of $36,000 to $39,000, depending on amount of experience and the setting. Certified rehabilitation counselors have slightly higher median salaries. In 2007, the range was $40,000 to $45,000, again, depending on the work setting.

As you gain more experience and move into supervisory roles, you can expect your salary to increase. In 2007, the median salary for directors of rehabilitation services ranged from $72,000 to $77,000, depending on the setting.

If you decide to go to medical school and become a rehabilitation physician, the median salary range is between $135,000 and $153,000, depending on where you work. In 2007, physicians in private practice had a median income of $143,000.

Pursuing your education and getting certified or licensed in your chosen field are the way to higher income levels within the field of rehabilitation services. The chapters that follow will provide more detail on salaries for specific positions and how to qualify for them. Taking one step at a time and continuing your education at every step are the best methods to increase your salary and advance in this field.

ADVANCING IN YOUR CAREER AS A REHABILITATION COUNSELOR

Like any career field, there are career paths within the field of rehabilitation services. However, advancement depends on what you consider to be your strength and love in the field. With increased levels of education and increased years of experience working directly with clients and patients, rehabilitation counselors can become supervisors of others who provide direct counseling services. From that position, they can also become program or agency directors, where they have responsibility for planning and implementing programs, hiring and training staff, and planning and managing budgets. In this capacity, rehabilitation counseling professionals rarely provide services directly to clients and patients.

While becoming a supervisor or director is an advancement, so is remaining in direct service to clients and patients where the complexity of the caseload requires higher levels of skill and knowledge. Other methods for advancing within the field of rehabilitation counseling include starting in a small program or organization and moving to a larger agency, either as a counselor with a client and patient caseload or as a supervisor or director.

Those who obtain a doctorate in rehabilitation counseling or a related area can teach and conduct research at the college or university level. As mentioned earlier, others go into private practice alone or as a member of a group of practitioners.

ADDITIONAL SOURCES OF INFORMATION

American Association for Marriage and Family Therapy
112 S. Alfred St.
Alexandria, VA 22314-3061
http://aamft.org/index_nm.asp

American Counseling Association
5999 Stevenson Ave.
Alexandria, VA 22304
counseling.org

American Rehabilitation Counseling Association
5999 Stevenson Ave.
Alexandria, VA 22304
arcaweb.org

Association for Education and Rehabilitation of the Blind and Visually
  Impaired
1703 N. Beauregard St., Suite 440
Alexandria, VA 22311
http://aerbvi.org

Association on Higher Education and Disability (AHEAD)
107 Commerce Center Dr., Suite 204
Huntersville, NC 28078
ahead.org

The Canadian Association of Rehabilitation Professionals, Inc.
302–201 Consumers Rd.
Toronto, ON M2J 4G8
Canada
carpnational.org

Chi Sigma Iota
P.O. Box 35448
Greensboro, NC 27425-5448
csi-net.org
Chi Sigma Iota is the international honor society for students, professional counselors, and counselor educators. The mission is to promote scholarship, research, professionalism, leadership, and excellence in counseling and to recognize high attainment in the pursuit of academic and clinical excellence in the profession of counseling.

Commission on Rehabilitation Counselor Certification
300 N. Martingale Rd., Suite 460
Schaumburg, IL 60173
crccertification.com

Council on Rehabilitation Education
300 N. Martingale Rd., Suite 460
Schaumburg, IL 60173
core-rehab.org

International Association of Rehabilitation Professionals (IARP)
1926 Waukegan Rd., Suite 1
Glenview, IL 60025-1770
rehabpro.org

National Board for Certified Counselors (NBCC)
3 Terrace Way
Greensboro, NC 27403-3660
http://nbcc.org

National Council on Rehabilitation Education
2012 W. Norwood Dr.
Carbondale, IL 62901
rehabeducators.org

National Rehabilitation Association
633 S. Washington St.
Alexandria, VA 22314
nationalrehab.org

National Rehabilitation Counseling Association
P.O. Box 4480
Manassas, VA 20108
http:nrca-net.org

SOCIAL WORK

Did you know that social workers are the nation's largest group of mental health services providers? In fact, the National Association of Social Workers reports that there are more clinically trained social workers than psychiatrists, psychologists, and psychiatric nurses combined.

The field of social work has deep roots in the United States, dating back to the establishment of Hull House in Chicago in the late 1880s. Jane Addams, the founder of Hull House and the first American woman to receive the Nobel Prize for Peace, was committed to improving the quality of life for people suffering from poverty, illness, and other life crises. Today, social workers continue to represent the principles and philosophy set forth by Jane Addams.

More than 600,000 social workers contribute to the improved welfare of a wide variety of people in the United States. It is a popular notion that social workers are all caseworkers in cities and municipal governments. While many do work in the area of public assistance, there are many other settings in which social workers contribute their expertise and their concern for humanity.

THE NATURE OF THE WORK

Social workers help people cope with diverse problems, from antisocial behavior to financial management. Social workers usually specialize in a specific area. The National Association of Social Work lists forty-two areas in which social workers practice. They include the following:

Mental health therapy	Community mental health
Disaster relief	Employee assistance
Military social work	Private practice
Rural social work	Veterans services
Adoption and foster care	Child abuse and neglect
Child welfare services	Domestic violence
Family preservation services	Political development
Homeless family assistance	Parent education
Eating disorders	Family planning
Genetics	HIV/AIDS
Hospital social work	School alternative programs
Crisis intervention	Difficulties in school
School violence	Gerontology services
Hospice and palliative care	Community-based services
Depression	In-home services
Institutional care	Senile dementia and Alzheimer's
Chronic pain	Addictions prevention/ treatment
Outpatient treatment	Criminal justice
Development disabilities	Housing assistance
International social work	Public welfare
Advocacy, consulting, and planning	Employment services

In Canada, the Canadian Association of Social Workers (CASW) recently created a Health Interest Group, Children's Issues Interest Group, and Aboriginal Social Workers Interest Group among its members. This doesn't mean that Canadian social workers only work in these areas. Like their U.S. counterparts, they work in a variety of settings and a range of specializations.

Through direct counseling and coordination of services, social workers help clients in these areas identify and consider solutions. The coordination of services for clients is a hallmark of the social work profession.

While there is some overlap, the way that social workers conduct their work can be grouped into three categories.

Casework

In this category the social worker is primarily involved in one-on-one counseling with the client. Some examples would include the following:

- Helping a client handle an abusive situation
- Identifying needed medical care, education and training, and homemaking services for a client
- Helping a client adjust to a traumatic injury or illness
- Counseling a patient's family

Group Work

In this category the social worker is primarily involved in counseling and working with groups of people. Some examples would include the following:

- Conducting job-seeking strategies for workers who have been laid off
- Teaching courses in child care for teenage parents
- Working with street gangs to prevent crime
- Conducting group counseling sessions for cancer patients
- Helping groups of people with the same issues find resolution

Community Organization Work

In this category the social worker is primarily involved in outreach to other community organizations in an attempt to identify resources and support for clients served by the agency. Some examples would include the following:

- Working with child advocacy groups to find foster homes
- Identifying resources to assist families affected by floods, tornadoes, hurricanes, and other natural disasters
- Coordinating funds and services from the government to serve a local need
- Working in conjunction with the juvenile court

THE WORK OF SOCIAL WORKERS

The profession of social work addresses the human needs of all members of society. Individual social workers usually specialize in the types of people with whom they wish to work. There are at least seven specializations in the field of social work.

Child Welfare or Family Services

These social workers assist parents and guardians in identifying services to improve the quality of life for children and families. They can also investigate cases of reported abuse and neglect. These social workers become involved in such things as crisis intervention, outreach, and individual and group counseling.

Medical

These social workers are members of the medical team composed of doctors, nurses, and therapists that develops treatment plans to help patients cope with chronic or terminal illness and injury. Some social workers specialize within this group as well. They may focus on the needs of transplant, heart attack, cancer, AIDS, or Alzheimer's patients.

School

These social workers help parents, teachers, and students cope with the special problems of children in elementary, middle, or high school. The issues can range from cases of suspected abuse to arranging for other social services to improve the overall quality of life so that the children can get the most from their education.

Community

These social workers become involved in many aspects of a local community including public welfare, housing, and the criminal justice system. Many social workers in this area work with the victims of poverty to assist them in identifying community resources for which they are eligible. Others work with the court system to provide services to juvenile offenders and prison inmates. Some become involved in pre-sentencing investigations of convicted criminals, and others become involved in the investigations of custody suits.

Clinical

These social workers participate in the treatment of patients under the care of psychiatrists and psychologists in mental health institutions. Chapter 6 provides more detailed information about this particular area of social work.

Industry

These social workers are usually members of the human resources departments of business and industry and address such issues as improved productivity, worker safety, employee turnover, and chronic absenteeism.

Gerontological Services

These social workers are part of a new and emerging field of social work. As the population ages, there is an increasing need to assist the elderly in obtaining appropriate medical, social, and recreational services.

WHERE SOCIAL WORKERS WORK

Federal, state, provincial, and local agencies employ many social workers. These organizations are devoted to such diverse issues as social services, child welfare, mental health, physical health, housing, public welfare, education, human resources, military, and corrections.

Other social workers are employed in nonprofit social service organizations as well as community and religious programs. Hospitals, rehab centers, recreation programs, nursing homes, and home health agencies also hire social workers. Some social workers are employed in business and industry, and others, who are licensed, enter private practice in their communities.

HOW TO QUALIFY TO BECOME A SOCIAL WORKER

In order to carry out their responsibilities, social workers must have a strong knowledge of human development and behavior, as well as a broad knowledge of how social, economic, and cultural institutions interact. That is why only people who hold bachelor's, master's, or doctoral degrees in social work can be called social workers. They must have a strong educational background to serve their clients. Like rehabilitation counselors, most social workers have a master's degree in social work.

A bachelor's degree in social work, rehabilitation services, sociology, psychology, or another social science is good preparation for the master's degree in social work (M.S.W.). Graduate courses in social work include human growth and development, social welfare policies, and methods of social work. The M.S.W. requires at least one year of clinical experience in an agency, hospital, or school under the direct supervision of an experienced M.S.W.

After two years of supervised experience, social workers are eligible for membership in the Academy of Certified Social Workers.

The Council on Social Work Education (CSWE) website (http://portal
.cswe.org/membership/memberdirectlrysearch.aspx) provides an up-to-date list of accredited schools of social work in the United States. On the website, you can enter the city and/or state in which you want to study and whether you are pursuing a bachelor's or master's degree and you will get a list of all the accredited programs in that area. In addition, CSWE provides a list of scholarships that are available to eligible students of social work. That website is www.cswe.org/cswe/scholarships. The Canadian Association for Schools of Social Work (cassw-acess.ca) provides a similar list of schools in Canada. (Note the spelling is CASSW-ACESS.)

WHAT CAN YOU EARN AS A SOCIAL WORKER?

Like that for rehabilitation counselors, the median salary for social workers is very modest. According to a 2007 survey conducted by PayScale.com, the median salary for social workers with one year or less of work experience was $26,921. This means that half of those participating in the salary survey made more than $26,921 and half made less. For social workers with five to nine years of experience, the median salary was $35,556.

Depending on the setting in which social workers are employed, salaries can vary. For example, in 2007 social workers employed in hospitals had a median salary of $38,000. Social workers employed by nonprofit organizations had a median salary of $31,500, and those employed by state and local governments earned a median salary of $35,500. Federal government agencies paid a median salary of $36,500.

ADVANCING IN YOUR CAREER AS A SOCIAL WORKER

According to the United States Bureau of Labor Statistics, the "employment of social workers is expected to increase faster than the average through 2014." This means that there will be opportunities for advancement, if you have the required education and experience.

Like rehabilitation counselors, social workers are able to advance to supervisory and administrative positions. Those with the advanced education and experience can be promoted to supervisor of caseworkers or director of an agency. It is also possible to move from a small agency to a larger one and assume more responsibility.

As in the case of rehabilitation counselors, an increasing number of social workers are becoming certified and licensed. Many establish private practices, either alone or with a larger group of professionals.

ADDITIONAL SOURCES OF INFORMATION

American Federation of State, County, and Municipal Employees
1625 L St. NW
Washington, DC 20036
afscme.org

Canadian Association of Schools of Social Work
1398 ch. Star Top Rd.
Ottawa, ON K13 4V7
Canada
cassw-acess.ca

Canadian Association of Social Workers (CASW)
383 Parkdale Ave., Suite 402
Ottawa, ON K1Y 4R4
Canada
casw-acts.ca

CASW Member Organizations

Alberta College of Social Workers
#550, 10707 100 Ave. NW
Edmonton, AB T5J 3M1
Canada
acsw.ab.ca

Association of Social Workers
1755 W. Broadway, Suite 402
Vancouver, BC V6J 4S5
Canada
bcasw.org

The Association of Social Workers of Northern Canada
Box 2963
Yellowknife, NT X1A 2R2
Canada
socialworknorth.com

Council on Social Work Education
1725 Duke St., Suite 500
Alexandria, VA 22314
cswe.org

Manitoba Association of Social Workers
Unit 4, 2015 Portage Ave.
Winnipeg, MB R3J 0K3
Canada
maswmirsw.ca

The Manitoba Institute of Registered Social Workers
maswmirsw.ca

National Association of Social Workers
750 First St. NE, Suite 700
Washington, DC 20002-4241
naswdc.org

New Brunswick Association of Social Workers
P.O. Box 1533, Postal Station A
Fredericton, NS E3B 5G2
Canada
nbasw-atsnb.ca

Newfoundland and Labrador Association of Social Workers
P.O. Box 39039
St. John's, NL A1E 5Y7
Canada
nlasw.ca

Nova Scotia Association of Social Workers
1891 Brunswick St., Suite 106
Halifax, NS B3J 2G8
Canada
nsasw.org

Ontario Association of Social Workers
410 Jarvis St.
Toronto, ON M4Y 2G6
Canada
oasw.org

Prince Edward Island Association of Social Workers
81 Prince St.
Charlottetown, PE C1A 4R3
Canada

Saskatchewan Association of Social Workers
2110 Lorne St.
Regina, SK S4P 2M5
Canada
sasw.ca

CHAPTER

5

EMPLOYMENT SERVICES

In our society, we define ourselves by the work that we do. Work is so important to us that we even ask young children what they want to be when they grow up. Work gives us a sense of purpose. When the ability to continue to do our work or find appropriate work for our talents is lost, social and rehabilitation services professionals provide assistance in obtaining employment and training to a variety of people in a variety of circumstances.

Disabling conditions such as developmental disabilities, strokes, heart attacks, cancer, and injury can prevent a person from pursuing work that is both financially and psychologically satisfying.

For example, soldiers injured by explosive devices in Iraq and Afghanistan are often not able to continue in the jobs or professions that they had before the war. This can have profound consequences on their psychological well-being, as well as on their families.

Many studies have shown that the loss of a job is almost as traumatic as the death of a spouse or a child. Consequently, the professionals in rehabilitation services who work with people who have vocational and employment challenges are doing important work in helping those people contribute to society and develop a sense of purpose about their lives.

There are many occupations related to employment services in the field of rehabilitation services, and the future demand for these professionals is tied very closely to the changing nature of the workplace and government legislation. In recent years, these two factors have opened opportunities for people with disabilities. That means that there is an increasing need for professionals who can assist special populations in entering the workforce in new numbers.

In addition, the workplace of the future will demand a new level of technology-related skills. Business and industry will look to employment service professionals to substantiate the skill level of each applicant.

VOCATIONAL EVALUATOR

People who suffer unexpected physical and mental disabilities often need to change their occupations. They have a need for knowledge about how their work-related skills can be transferred to a new occupation. The expertise of vocational evaluators in vocational/career testing and goal setting is important in making that transition.

The Work of the Vocational Evaluator

Vocational evaluators measure and assess the vocational interests, knowledge, and skills of individuals seeking to perform certain jobs. The individuals served by vocational evaluators might include physically and mentally disabled clients as well as healthy ones. It is important that vocational evaluators be knowledgeable about the reliability of interest, aptitude, and achievement tests related to specific jobs.

These professionals measure and evaluate skills in a variety of job areas. They can test a person's knowledge and ability in such areas as keyboarding, computer hardware and software, mathematical and analytical ability, and industrial and technological expertise. They can also evaluate an individual's ability to use certain types of office or industrial equipment. And, they test a person's interest in specific occupational areas.

Some vocational evaluators can be responsible for placing their clients in work settings and monitoring their progress. In these positions, vocational evaluators work closely with local businesses and industries. Some vocational evaluators work together with other professionals to serve as advocates for these clients. The advocates can include such people as teachers, counselors, therapists, and physicians.

As stated earlier, the primary group of people served by vocational evaluators includes physically and mentally disabled clients. They can also include groups such as laid-off or unemployed workers, high school dropouts, teenage mothers, workers injured on the job, and displaced homemakers.

In addition to the people whom vocational evaluators serve, they often interact with other professionals. They confer with lawyers, insurance companies, employers, health-care professionals, and other career counselors.

Where Vocational Evaluators Work

Vocational evaluators work in a variety of settings. Some of these settings are rehabilitation centers, public and private schools, community colleges, trade schools, community agencies, employment centers, private businesses, and labor unions.

Some vocational evaluators are self-employed. They maintain private practices to evaluate individuals for specialized training programs or specific jobs.

How to Qualify to Become a Vocational Evaluator

A college degree is a minimum requirement. Many positions now require a master's degree in a counseling-related area. Some vocational evaluators must be licensed by the state in which they work. In these cases, it might be necessary to have graduated from an accredited graduate program.

Course work in testing and measurement is highly desirable. An in-depth knowledge of testing methods and test interpretation is an important job requirement today. The legal responsibilities of vocational evaluators make their work extremely important to both their clients and their employer.

Each state has its own licensing requirements for vocational evaluators to become self-employed. Individuals interested in this career opportunity should confer with the state board for licensing and certification of professionals.

What Can You Earn as a Vocational Evaluator?

Depending on geographic location, employment setting, and years of experience, vocational evaluators' salaries can range from $25,000 to $45,000 per year.

How to Advance in Your Career as a Vocational Evaluator

According to Mississippi State University's Rehabilitation Research and Training Center on Blindness and Low Vision, "there is a good employment outlook for vocational evaluators who have expertise in all disability areas." Therefore, there are opportunities for vocational evaluators to advance in their careers. Because of the quantitative nature of their expertise, vocational evaluators are in demand.

Experienced vocational evaluators can assume supervisory and administrative positions in large agencies. In these settings, the vocational evaluator has responsibility for a team of evaluators. Other vocational evaluators who have gained increasing amounts of experience and who have pursued higher levels of education can move into counseling, therapeutic, or administrative positions. Experience and education greatly expand the vocational evaluator's opportunities for advancement.

VOCATIONAL REHABILITATION COUNSELOR

In a fast-paced world and a global economy, helping people with disabilities obtain and keep good jobs is increasingly important. Vocational rehabilitation counselors are an important part of this process. They provide clients and patients with access to a network of employers in the community and the tools to make informed decisions.

The Work of a Vocational Rehabilitation Counselor

The sudden loss of the ability to perform a job due to an accident or an illness can be very traumatic. Vocational rehabilitation counselors help people handle the impact of disabilities on their jobs and careers. Vocational rehabilitation counselors not only work with individuals who have suddenly suffered a loss of ability, but they also work with people who have congenital and developmental disabilities.

After conferring with their clients, vocational rehabilitation counselors develop and implement educational and support programs to increase their clients' employability. They help their clients make wise vocational decisions. Therefore, they must have a good understanding of their clients' potential as well as the skills that are in demand and the training programs available to prepare them for the job market.

Vocational rehabilitation counselors work with individuals who are old enough to enter the workforce. Consequently, they do not work with young children. The clients of vocational rehabilitation counselors have physical, mental, and/or emotional barriers that can inhibit their full participation in a job or career.

Some counselors specialize in serving a particular type of client. For example, some might work with the blind or the hearing impaired. In these areas, counselors might do as much work with employers as with the client. They can help the employer adapt the work environment to accommodate a hearing- or sight-impaired employee. Likewise, they work with clients to prepare them for the expectations of the workplace.

Other vocational rehabilitation counselors work with the mentally or emotionally disabled clients who have suffered the loss of their capacity to continue in a career field because of injury or illness. In these instances, the counselor usually needs to interact with others such as occupational therapists, special education teachers, and the client's family.

Where Vocational Rehabilitation Counselors Work

Vocational rehabilitation counselors work in job training and vocational rehabilitation centers, state employment offices, veterans' programs, and colleges and universities. They also work in private and government-sponsored social service programs. While some vocational rehabilitation counselors are self-employed as private practice counselors, most work in agencies that provide free vocational counseling and job placement to disabled clients.

How to Qualify to Become a Vocational Rehabilitation Counselor

A master's degree in rehabilitation counseling is generally a minimum requirement. However, a master's degree in other counseling areas might be acceptable. These areas include, but are not limited to, counseling and guidance, mental health counseling, or counseling psychology in which course work in career counseling, individual appraisal, and occupational information was completed. In some small agencies and communities, people with a bachelor's degree in rehabilitation services, counseling services, psychology, or other related fields might be able to work with vocational rehabilitation clients.

What Can You Earn as a Vocational Rehabilitation Counselor?

According to the 2007 PayScale.com salary survey of vocational rehabilitation counselors, the median annual salary for an individual with one year or less of experience was $36,600. This means that half of the people who participated in the salary survey made more than $36,600 and half made less. For those with five to nine years of experience the median annual salary was $43,000.

Depending on the setting in which a vocational rehabilitation counselor works, the median annual salary can vary. In 2007, the median annual salaries paid in the following settings were:

State and local government	$41,000
Nonprofit organizations	$41,000
Federal government	$44,000
Private practice	$43,000

It is important to keep in mind that these median salaries are not starting salaries. They take into account all vocational rehabilitation counselors, whether they have less than one year of experience or more than twenty years of experience.

How to Advance in Your Career as a Vocational Rehabilitation Counselor

Overall, opportunities in vocational rehabilitation counseling are expected to grow faster than average. The more experience vocational rehabilitation counselors gain in vocational testing, career and employment counseling, and job development, the more opportunities they will have for advancement. Likewise, increased levels of education will qualify vocational rehabilitation counselors for supervisory and administrative positions within their current organizations or larger agencies.

Vocational rehabilitation counselors who aspire to administrative positions sometimes find it helpful to take graduate courses in public administration or business administration. These courses enhance their ability to prepare and defend agency budgets and to monitor the impact of federal, state, and local legislation and regulations on the agency and its clients.

CAREER COUNSELOR

According to the National Career Development Association, career counselors are professionals who are trained and certified to help clients "make and carry out decisions and plans related to life/career directions." Career counselors can also assist in managing careers and working to achieve a good work/life balance.

The Work of Career Counselors

Career counselors assist a wide range of people in making career decisions related to entering the workforce, reentering the workforce, or making a career change. While vocational rehabilitation counselors specialize in assisting persons with disabilities in making career decisions, career counselors generally work with a range of individuals who are faced with making career decisions.

Career counselors assist their clients in exploring and evaluating their education, specialized training, work history, career and personal interests, job skills, personal strengths and weaknesses, and physical capacities. To do this, career counselors often conduct or arrange for aptitude, achievement, and/or interest testing. They also spend a considerable amount of time working with their clients individually or in groups to help each person become more aware of his or her own potential, set more realistic career goals, and develop a plan of action to accomplish the goals.

In addition to counseling, career counselors can also become involved in teaching job-seeking individuals resume writing and job interviewing skills. They can also assist clients in applying and competing for jobs that match their preparation, skills, and interests.

Career counselors work with a range of people involved in making career and/or life decisions. The groups with whom career counselors work can range from elementary students who are becoming aware of the variety of career options through their schoolwork to laid-off workers who must now find new jobs or change career fields.

In some instances the clients of career counselors are not under pressure to make career decisions. However, most of the time career counselors are working with clients who are under a great deal of pressure. They can be college or high school students who must find a first job but who have not really thought through personal interests, strengths, needs, and goals. Or they can be displaced homemakers or widows who suddenly find that they need to enter or reenter the workforce but feel they have no marketable skills.

Career counselors often specialize in working with certain types of people who are making career decisions. However, unlike other occupations within employment services, career counselors can be generalists. Their knowledge of tests and measurement, vocational development stages, theories of decision making, occupational information, and the job market makes it easy for them to adapt to different groups of people over the course of their careers.

Where Career Counselors Work

Many career counselors work in public and private high schools and colleges. Career counselors are also employed in job training and vocational rehabilitation centers. Some community agencies and special programs employ career counselors to assist individuals who are affected by corporate downsizing and other shifts in the job market.

In recent years, some career counselors have been employed by government agencies, business organizations, and major industries to assist in retraining, promoting, and outplacing employees. Others have entered private practice to provide these services. Career counselors in private practice must meet appropriate licensing requirements in the area where they plan to work.

How to Qualify to Become a Career Counselor

The minimum requirement for a career counseling position is a master's degree in a counseling-related discipline. The areas of study most appropriate for career counseling positions are career counseling, counselor education, guidance and counseling, college student affairs, school counseling, rehabilitation counseling, and counseling psychology.

Graduation from a program accredited by the Council for Accreditation of Counseling and Related Educational Programs or the Council on Rehabilitation Education can be an important consideration for those planning to become certified or licensed. Because each state differs in its requirements, it is important to contact the appropriate board for licensure or certification.

What Can You Earn as a Career Counselor?

According to the 2007 PayScale.com salary survey of career counselors, the median annual salary for an individual with one year or less of experience was $31,500. This means that half of the people who participated in the survey made more than $31,500 and half made less. For those with five to nine years of experience, the median annual salary was $40,000.

Depending on the setting in which a career counselor works, median annual salary can vary. In 2007, the median annual salaries paid in the following settings were:

College	$40,000
Public schools	$38,000
Nonprofit organizations	$38,000
Federal government	$41,000
State and local government	$38,500
Company	$40,000

It is important to keep in mind that these median salaries are not starting salaries. They take into account all career counselors, whether they have less than one year of experience or more than twenty years of experience.

How to Advance in Your Career as a Career Counselor

Like other counseling careers, the job opportunities for career counselors are expected to grow faster than average. However, advancement will differ from other types of counseling because of the variety of settings in which career counseling is carried out. For example, career counselors who are employed in public school systems can become directors of guidance for their school or supervisors of guidance for their school district or state.

Career counselors employed in colleges and universities can become directors of career services centers. Some career counselors in higher education and in industry have been promoted to the position of vice president for student affairs in colleges or vice president of human resources in business and industry.

Those who obtain a doctorate can become counselor educators and teach or perform research in colleges and universities. Others can pass state licensing requirements and go into private practice. Still others may develop a consulting practice serving educational and employment organizations.

SUPPORTED EMPLOYMENT COORDINATOR

Supported employment programs serve people with an array of disabilities. These programs operate with the belief that all people have the potential to work, but some people need extra support to learn and adapt to their job. Supported employment coordinators not only identify and develop jobs for their clients, they also work as job coaches to help them learn the job and succeed in it.

The Work of a Supported Employment Coordinator

Supported employment has become the newest method of providing employment and training opportunities for persons with severe disabilities. In the past, sheltered workshops provided the only opportunities that these individuals had for learning job-related skills.

Sheltered workshops were operated by institutions where adolescents and adults with severe disabilities lived. For example, in Chicago, one of the nation's largest nonprofit providers of mental health services, Thresholds (thresholds.org), provides a comprehensive program of therapeutic support, case management, education, job training and placement, and housing for people with mental illness. One of the work programs is Urban

Meadows, a nonprofit florist, which provides opportunities for their clients to learn and use floral design skills. The Urban Meadows shop is located in the heart of Chicago's financial district, which has greatly contributed to its success. These types of organizations provide an opportunity for adolescents and adults to experience the rewards of the regular workplace.

Today the emphasis is on providing supported employment environments for people with severe disabilities. This can mean training and supervising clients in paid jobs in regular work settings or operating commercial enterprises, like Urban Meadows, in the community. Within these commercial enterprises, small groups of clients provide a service or do assembly work for local businesses.

There are four models for supported employment.

1. **Supported job model.** This program places adults and adolescents in regular jobs in the community and provides training and support. At each work site, there is a job coach for each worker. The job coach teaches the person how to perform the job.

2. **Enclave model.** This program places a small group of people (five to six) with severe to moderate disabilities in regular assembly jobs in business and industry to work with normal workers. A job coach and a trained employee of the business or industry are present to teach the members of the group how to do the job.

3. **Mobile crew model.** This program is so named because the community agency establishes a business to provide services to local business and industry under contract. Small groups of disabled workers are taken to each job site to perform such functions as groundskeeping and janitorial services.

4. **Benchwork.** The community agency operates a small, single-purpose nonprofit corporation, which performs a function under contract to individuals and/or businesses. Examples of this type of work can be stripping furniture or routine assembly work.

It is the supported employment coordinator's responsibility to identify and analyze these types of jobs and businesses to determine their suitability for the special population to be served.

The clients in supported employment need intensive, ongoing supervision and training to do each job. In small programs, the supported employment coordinator can also provide the individual training and supervision at the job site. In larger programs, that function is performed by the mental retardation (MR) job coach.

Supported employment coordinators work with a diverse group of people. In addition to working with severely to moderately retarded adults and adolescents, they also work with public officials and with businesspeople in the community.

To support participating employers as well as individuals with severe disabilities, supported employment coordinators interact with other social services professionals to identify needed resources in the community.

Where Supported Employment Coordinators Work

While a few supported employment coordinators are employed by industry, the majority are employed by nonprofit community agencies. These agencies get most of their funding from governmental sources, at all levels.

In addition to spending time in the agency, much of the supported employment coordinator's time is spent in business and industry. It is there that the supported employment counselor either develops job opportunities or trains and supervises clients.

How to Qualify to Become a Supported Employment Coordinator

Usually an undergraduate degree in social work, special education, or a closely related field is required to become a supported employment coordinator. In addition, most employers would like at least one year of experience working directly with people with disabilities or job placement. This can be accomplished through volunteer work, summer jobs, and internships required in your academic program.

In some cases, supported employment coordinators are hired without a college degree, but some college education is required. In these cases, at least three years of experience in job placement, preferably for persons with developmental disabilities, is required.

All supported employment coordinators need to be knowledgeable about a variety of agencies. They must also have strong oral and written communication skills because their jobs require clear communication in phone calls, coaching, and visits to employers, as well as writing and responding in e-mails, letters, and reports. Public speaking is also important because supported employment coordinators provide training sessions for employers hiring the developmentally disabled. Flexibility is also vital. Supported employment coordinators must be willing to work varied hours. Many of their placements are in the retail and fast-food industries, which have early morning and late night hours. The supported employment coordinator is needed on the job, with the client, in order to teach the tasks necessary for the client to be successful.

What Can You Earn as a Supported Employment Coordinator?

Individuals in rehabilitation services jobs such as supported employment coordinators earned a median annual salary of $24,270 in 2004, according to the U.S. Bureau of Labor Statistics. The top 10 percent of those surveyed earned more than $39,620, and the lowest 10 percent earned less than $15,480.

How to Advance in Your Career as a Supported Employment Coordinator

Between now and 2014, the job growth outlook for supported employment coordinators is expected to be faster than average. Therefore, the more experience supported employment coordinators gain, the more opportunities they will have for advancement. Likewise, increasing levels of education qualify them for supervisory and higher-level administrative positions within their current organizations or in larger agencies.

Supported employment coordinators who aspire to administrative positions sometimes find it helpful to take graduate course work in public administration or business administration. This preparation enhances their ability to prepare and defend agency budgets and to monitor the impact of federal, state, and local legislation and regulations on their agency and clients. Courses in business administration give supported employment counselors a better understanding of the needs and demands of the businesses and industries with which they work.

MENTAL RETARDATION (MR) JOB COACH

According to the Office of Disability Employment Policy of the U.S. Department of Labor, "Mental retardation begins in childhood and is characterized by limitations in both intelligence and adaptive skills. Mental retardation is diagnosed based on three criteria: 1.) intellectual functioning (IQ) below 70–75; 2.) significant limitations in two or more adaptive skill areas and 3.) the condition is present from childhood, defined as age 18 or less." People who have been diagnosed with mental retardation can require more and different support in the workplace. A job coach, specially trained to work with the mentally retarded, can provide the one-on-one job training, positive feedback, and meaningful rewards to help their client contribute in the workplace.

The Work of the MR Job Coach

MR job coaches are important members of the supported employment program. They motivate and prepare severely to moderately mentally retarded clients to work in jobs outside of the residential institution. The MR job coach works with each employer to identify all of the steps in a job and carefully designs an individually tailored training process to teach the job to a client.

In most cases the MR job coach learns the job and performs the job for the employer for a brief time before bringing the client to the work site. When the special worker arrives at the job, the MR job coach is there until it is certain that the individual can perform the job without constant supervision. This process can take weeks or months depending on the individual and the severity of the disability.

The MR job coach returns on a regular basis to check on the individual and his or her job performance. The caseload for most MR job coaches is only four to six individuals because of the time-consuming nature of the training and supervision.

MR job coaches generally work with severely to moderately retarded adults and adolescents. Occasionally, they also work with people with severe physical disabilities. They also work closely with employers and their regular employees. It is important that the MR job coach identify a model worker from among the regular employees. This individual works closely with the MR job coach to train the client and to learn about the capabilities and limitations of the individual's disability. When the MR job coach no longer comes regularly, the model worker assumes the supervision of the special worker on a day-to-day basis.

Where MR Job Coaches Work

MR job coaches are employed by nonprofit community agencies that serve severely to moderately disabled individuals. However, most of their time is spent in the community on regular job sites. Their clients might only work three to six hours per day, but the preparation time requires that the MR job coach spend much more time than that at the work sites.

In general, service industries tend to be the primary employers in supported employment programs. Therefore, the MR job coach is likely to be working in restaurants, hotels, and offices.

How to Qualify to Become an MR Job Coach

A college degree is generally required. A bachelor's degree in rehabilitation services, social work, sociology, psychology, special education, or a related field would be considered the most appropriate preparation.

What Can You Earn as an MR Job Coach?

Individuals working as MR job coaches earned a median annual salary of $20,400 in 2004, according to the U.S. Bureau of Labor Statistics. The top 10 percent of those surveyed earned more than $39,620, and the lowest 10 percent earned less than $15,480.

How to Advance in Your Career as an MR Job Coach

Because jobs as MR job coaches are expected to grow faster than average, there are opportunities for MR job coaches to become supported employment coordinators or supervisors of other MR job coaches. They can go to a larger community agency where responsibilities will increase. Like almost every occupation in this category, the more education and experience a person has, the more opportunities there will be for advancement.

ADDITIONAL SOURCES OF INFORMATION

American Counseling Association
5999 Stevenson Ave.
Alexandria, VA 22304
counseling.org

Association for Career and Technical Education
1410 King St.
Alexandria, VA 22314
acteonline.org

The Canadian Career Development Foundation
119 Ross Ave., Suite 202
Ottawa, ON K1Y 0N6
Canada
ccdf.ca/ccdf2

Canadian Employee Assistance Program Association
1031 Portage Ave.
Winnipeg, MB R3G 0R8
Canada
ceapa.ca/index.htm

Canadian Professional Counsellors Association
3306 32nd Ave. #203
Vernon, BC V1T 2M6
Canada
cpca-rpc.ca

Career Planning and Adult Development Network
543 Vista Mar Ave.
Pacifica, CA 94044 USA
careernetwork.org

Commission on Rehabilitation Counselor Certification
300 N. Martingale Rd., Suite 460
Schaumburg, IL 60173
crccertification.com

Council for Accreditation of Counseling and Related Educational
   Programs
1001 N. Fairfax St., Suite 510
Alexandria, VA 22314
cacrep.org

National Board for Certified Counselors
3 Terrace Way
Greensboro, NC 27403
nbcc.org

National Career Development Association
305 N. Beech Cir.
Broken Arrow, OK 74012
ncda.org

National Employment Counseling Association
5999 Stevenson Ave.
Alexandria, VA 22304
employmentcounseling.org/neca.html

C H A P T E R

6

MENTAL HEALTH SERVICES

At times everyone is confronted by personal, professional, and social problems. Often these problems seem insurmountable. Therefore, it is not surprising that every year more than 30 million people seek the help of mental health professionals.

These professionals use a variety of approaches to help their clients and patients deal with issues related to mental and emotional health. They also work in a range of settings where their work can be both physically and emotionally demanding. However, all of these professionals have one thing in common—they are committed to promoting optimum mental health for their clients and patients.

PSYCHIATRIC SOCIAL WORKER

According to the National Association of Social Workers (NASW), all social workers "help clients deal not only with how they feel about a situation but also with what they can do about it." Psychiatric social workers are mental health professionals who are highly trained to understand and help clients with the many factors that impact mental disorders. These professionals possess master's degrees in social work (M.S.W.) and are usually licensed clinical social workers (LCSW).

The Work of Psychiatric Social Workers

The field of social work offers a variety of career options. One of the most important branches is the field of psychiatric social work. Psychiatric social workers are an integral part of most mental health teams, which are made up of psychiatrists, therapists, nurses, and counselors. They often serve as the liaison between the patients and their families and the psychiatrists or psychologists. In some cases, the psychiatric social worker can also serve as the ombudsman between the hospital and the patient and/or the family when misunderstandings occur.

Psychiatric social workers gather data about the patient and the circumstances in which the patient lives. They prepare family histories and conduct interviews of all parties who play a significant role in the life of the patient. All of this information is vital in planning the overall treatment program.

Some aspects of the treatment program can be provided by the psychiatric social worker. In addition, it is often the psychiatric social worker who explains the treatments and their purpose to the patient and the family. These treatments can include individual, group, and/or family counseling as well as medical intervention.

Psychiatric social workers generally work with patients who have been hospitalized with mental or emotional disorders. They can also work with the families of the patients.

Some psychiatric social workers specialize in certain types of mental illness and/or certain types of people with mental and emotional disabilities. For example, a psychiatric social worker might work exclusively with autistic children or with adult schizophrenics or with the criminally insane.

Psychiatric social workers interact professionally with physicians, therapists, nurses, and mental health counselors. Sometimes they are supervised by other psychiatric social workers. However, most often they are supervised directly by psychiatrists or psychologists.

Where Psychiatric Social Workers Work

While psychiatric social workers might work for the same agencies and institutions as other social workers, most are employed by hospitals or mental health agencies where they work in psychiatric units.

other medical facilities. Still others go into private practice. Often this is a group practice with a team of other mental health professionals.

How to Qualify to Become a Psychiatric Social Worker

Psychiatric social workers must have a master's degree in social work with a specialization in psychiatric social work. This is in addition to the traditional graduate courses in human growth and development, social welfare policies, and methods of social work. This specialization requires a heavy concentration of course work in psychology.

All graduate students in social work are required to do at least one year of clinical experience in an agency, hospital, or school under the direct supervision of an experienced M.S.W. However, psychiatric social work students must complete their clinical experience under the direct supervision of psychiatrists or clinical psychologists.

Like other social workers, the psychiatric social worker is eligible for membership in the Academy of Certified Social Workers after two years of supervised experience. This certification and state license qualify the psychiatric social worker to enter private practice.

What Can You Earn as a Psychiatric Social Worker?

The 2007 salary survey conducted by PayScale.com reported that the median salary for M.S.W. social workers with one year or less of work experience was $35,000. This means that half of the M.S.W.s participating in the salary survey made more than $35,000 and half made less. For M.S.W. social workers with five to nine years of experience, the median salary was $40,000.

Depending on the setting in which psychiatric social workers are employed, salaries can vary. For example, the median annual salary for those working in hospitals is $43,000. In private practice, the median annual salary is $41,500.

How to Advance in Your Career as a Psychiatric Social Worker

As the population ages and the retirement of baby boom psychiatric social workers occurs, there will be a faster than average increase in demand for these professionals through 2014. As a result, there will be increased opportunities for advancement to supervisory positions. Those with the proper education and experience might be promoted to unit supervisors or program directors. It is also possible to move from a small hospital to a larger one and assume more responsibilities. Those who complete a doctorate might teach and conduct research in a university setting. In addition, social workers are often required to be licensed by the state in which they practice. Holding licensure as a social worker provides more opportunities for advancement.

Additional Sources of Information

American Federation of State, County, and Municipal Employees
1625 L St. NW
Washington, DC 20036
afscme.org

Canadian Association of Schools of Social Work
1398 ch. Star Top Rd.
Ottawa, ON K13 4V7
Canada
cassw-acess.ca

Canadian Association of Social Workers
383 Parkdale Ave., Suite 402
Ottawa, ON K1Y 4R4
Canada
casw-acts.ca

CASW Member Organizations

Alberta College of Social Workers
10707 100 Ave. NW #550
Edmonton, AB T5J 3M1
Canada
acsw.ab.ca

The Association of Social Workers of Northern
  Canada
Box 2963
Yellowknife, NT X1A 2R2
Canada
socialworknorth.com

British Columbia Association of Social Workers
1755 W. Broadway, Suite 402
Vancouver, BC V6J 4S5
Canada
bcasw.org

Council on Social Work Education
1725 Duke St., Suite 500
Alexandria, VA 22314
cswe.org

Manitoba Association of Social Workers
Unit 4, 2015 Portage Ave.
Winnipeg, MB R3J 0K3
Canada
maswmirsw.ca

The Manitoba Institute of Registered Social Workers
maswmirsw.ca

National Association of Social Workers
750 First St. NE, Suite 700
Washington, DC 20002-4241
naswdc.org

New Brunswick Association of Social Workers
P.O. Box 1533, Postal Station A
Fredericton, NB E3B 5G2
Canada
nbasw-atsnb.ca

Newfoundland and Labrador Association of
    Social Workers
P.O. Box 39039
St. John's, NL A1E 5Y7
Canada
nlasw.ca

Nova Scotia Association of Social Workers
1891 Brunswick St., Suite 106
Halifax, NS B3J 2G8
Canada
nsasw.org

Ontario Association of Social Workers
410 Jarvis St.
Toronto, ON M4Y 2G6
Canada
oasw.org

Prince Edward Island Association of Social Workers
81 Prince St.
Charlottetown, PE C1A 4R3
Canada

Saskatchewan Association of Social Workers
2110 Lorne St.
Regina, SK S4P 2M5
Canada
sasw.ca

MENTAL HEALTH COUNSELOR

The National Academy of Certified Clinical Mental Health Counselors
(NACCMHC) defines clinical mental health counseling as "the provision
of professional counseling services, involving the application of principles

of psychotherapy, human development, learning theory, group dynamics, and the etiology of mental illness and dysfunctional behavior to individuals, couples, families and groups, for the purpose of treating psychopathology and promoting optimal mental health."

The Work of Mental Health Counselors

Mental health counselors use an array of counseling techniques to treat their clients. These techniques can include the following:

- Individual counseling
- Group therapy
- Outreach
- Crisis intervention
- Skills training in everyday living
- Social rehabilitation

Like the psychiatric social worker, mental health counselors are usually part of a mental health team. The other members generally include psychiatrists, psychologists, psychiatric nurses, and social workers. It is the goal of this team to restore full mental health to the patient, although this is not always possible.

Frequently mental health counselors specialize. They can concentrate in such areas as addiction and substance abuse, marriage and family problems, suicide prevention, stress management, problems of self-esteem, issues associated with aging, or vocational and educational decisions. As a specialist, the mental health counselor is able to provide more in-depth services to the patient.

As stated earlier, because mental health counselors can work with a range of individuals and groups, most specialize and work with specific groups. As a result, the other professionals with whom mental health counselors interact vary depending on the area of specialization.

For example, mental health counselors who work with public offenders primarily interact with the court system and officials in correctional institutions. Those who specialize in child abuse and neglect interact with family members, social workers, and medical professionals.

Where Mental Health Counselors Work

Like psychiatric social workers, most mental health counselors work in public or private mental hospitals or clinics. They can also work in the psychiatric units of comprehensive hospitals or in public and private mental health programs. With proper certification and licensure, some mental health counselors go into private practice. They might work alone or with a group of other mental health professionals.

How to Qualify to Become a Mental Health Counselor

Mental health counselors hold master's degrees in mental health counseling. However, there are some mental health counselors who hold master's degrees in psychology, social work, or a related counseling discipline. Increasingly, hospitals and clinics are requiring a Ph.D. in mental health counseling.

Mental health counselors are certified by the National Academy of Certified Clinical Mental Health Counselors. To become certified, mental health counselors must hold a master's degree and complete a period of supervised clinical experience, submit a taped sample of clinical work, pass a written examination, and complete two years of post-master's experience under the supervision of another certified mental health counselor.

What Can You Earn as a Mental Health Counselor?

Mental health counselors in their first year of work earned a median annual salary of $28,500 in 2007, according to PayScale.com. For those with five to nine years of experience, the median annual salary was $36,200.

Like other counseling specialties, the setting in which you work can make a difference in the median annual salary earned. The following list shows the median pay for mental health counselors in various settings.

Nonprofit organizations	$34,500
Schools and colleges	$34,500
State and local government agencies	$34,700
Hospitals	$36,000
Federal government agencies	$37,000
Private practice	$36,500

How to Advance in Your Career as a Mental Health Counselor

The demand for mental health counselors will continue to grow as more and more states implement networks of child and adolescent services. This means that more mental health counselors will be able to advance to directors or supervisors of counseling in the agencies that are implementing these networks. In addition, mental health counselors will still be able to move from small organizations to larger ones in order to assume leadership positions.

As in other areas of mental health services, mental health counselors who become certified and licensed in their state can enter private practice. Some who complete doctoral degrees teach and conduct research at colleges and universities.

Additional Sources of Information

American Mental Health Counselors Association
801 N. Fairfax St., Suite 304
Alexandria, VA 22314
amhca.org

Canadian Consortium for Collaborative Mental Health Care
    (CCCMHC)
10 George St., 3rd Floor
Hamilton, ON L8P 1C8
Canada
shared-care.ca

Canadian Mental Health Association
180 Dundas St. W., Suite 2301
Toronto, ON M5G 1Z8
Canada
cmha.ca/bins/index.asp

National Alliance on Mental Illness
Colonial Place Three
2107 Wilson Blvd., Suite 300
Arlington, VA 22201-3042
nami.org

SUBSTANCE ABUSE COUNSELOR

Substance abuse counselors work with people who suffer from chemical dependencies on drugs or alcohol. Most substance abuse counselors work as part of a team that includes professionals such as physicians, psychologists, social workers, and nurses who are dedicated to helping clients overcome addictions.

The Work of Substance Abuse Counselors

Substance abuse counselors are involved with individual and group counseling. They also participate in the evaluation of patients. In cases where pretreatment detoxification is warranted, the substance abuse counselors can refer the patient to an appropriate treatment facility.

Counselors in this area confront the patient with facts and information about his or her addiction. Because denial is a part of addiction, it is important that this confrontation be carried out in an instructional manner. Exhibiting a judgmental manner is not only unacceptable, it is counterproductive in the recovery process of addicts.

Many substance abuse counselors have either experienced addiction themselves or know people who are or have been addicted. This can give substance abuse counselors credibility with patients, particularly as they try to help the patient overcome denial. In these cases, substance abuse counselors use not only their expertise but also their experience with addiction to reach their patients.

Unfortunately young people, adults, and the elderly can all have problems with substance abuse. Addiction strikes all races and ethnic groups. Therefore, substance abuse counselors generally work with a wide range of people who suffer from the same problem. Some substance abuse counselors decide to specialize and work with particular groups of people. For example, some professionals might work only with teenagers and others only with public offenders.

On a professional level, substance abuse counselors must interact with medical personnel such as physicians, nurses, and therapists. Those who work in business and industry also work with the managers and supervisors of employees who have exhibited substance abuse problems that affect their work.

Where Substance Abuse Counselors Work

Generally the treatment programs are specialized. They address either alcohol or drug addiction. Within these specializations, there are usually further subdivisions depending on the characteristics of the client. For example, treatment programs differ for teenagers and for adults. Recently there has been recognition that new and different methods of treating women's addiction must be implemented. Treatment methods can differ for patients who seek help voluntarily or for those who are mandated to be in a treatment program by the courts or their employers.

Substance abuse counselors work in hospitals and in special treatment centers for persons with chemical addictions. Those who have advanced training, certification, and licensure might be in private practice. Sometimes the private practice is with a group of other health professionals who have specialized in the area of substance abuse.

How to Qualify to Become a Substance Abuse Counselor

In the past, substance abuse counselors have sometimes had little or no formal training. Typically they themselves had overcome addiction or had been close to people with chemical addictions. However, increasingly higher levels of specialized education and training are being required for entry into this field.

Now it is common for substance abuse counselors to have completed the same basic master's program as other counseling or social work professionals. However, they also do course work in the areas of therapy techniques associated with chemical addiction. Supervised internships are also common in the area of chemical dependency.

What Can You Earn as a Substance Abuse Counselor?

In 2007, the PayScale.com salary survey reported that the median salary for a substance abuse counselor with one year or less of work experience was $32,500. This means that half of the substance abuse counselors participating in the salary survey made more than $32,500 and half made less. For substance abuse counselors with five to nine years of experience, the median salary was $34,000.

Depending on the setting in which substance abuse counselors work, salaries can vary. For example, the median annual salary for those working in nonprofit agencies is $31,500, and in hospitals, it is $40,500. In private practice, the median annual salary is $37,900.

How to Advance in Your Career as a Substance Abuse Counselor

As we become more aware that treatment is a better way to address substance abuse than is jail time, the demand for substance abuse counselors is expected to be excellent for the future. As more treatment programs are opened, advancement opportunities will increase for substance abuse counselors.

Advancement in the field of substance abuse counseling is not unlike advancement in other areas of counseling and social work. Substance abuse counselors are able to advance to directors or supervisors of counseling in their agencies or hospitals. In other cases, they might move from small agencies to larger ones.

Those who obtain doctorates can also join the faculty of colleges and universities that teach and do research in the area of substance abuse counseling. Those who become certified and pass state licensing requirements can go into private practice. Others do research and consulting.

Additional Sources of Information

Canadian Network of Substance Abuse and Allied Professionals (CNSAAP)
75 Albert St., Suite 300
Ottawa, ON K1P 5E7
Canada
cnsaap.ca/cnsaap

National Clearinghouse on Alcoholism and Drug Abuse Information
P.O. Box 2345
Rockville, MD 20847
http://ncadi.samhsa.gov

National Institute on Drug Abuse
6001 Executive Blvd., Room 5213
Bethesda, MD 20892-9561
nida.nih.gov

PSYCHOLOGIST

Psychologists treat and observe individuals through testing, counseling, and controlled research experiments. Psychologists can also become involved in teaching and administration.

The Work of Psychologists

Psychologists are a very important group within mental health services. Their education and training prepare them to use a systematic approach to understanding and explaining human behavior. By using such methods as interviewing, testing, and observation, psychologists attempt to explain the needs and the behaviors of individuals and groups. As members of a mental health team, psychologists attend to the emotional and physical reactions of their patients.

In general, psychologists concentrate in one of the following specializations.

• **Clinical psychology.** This specialization focuses on the direct treatment of patients who have mental and emotional disorders. Clinical psychologists use a range of treatment techniques. These can include such things as psychoanalysis, behavior modification, or medication to help patients cope with the issues that confront them. In the United States there are more than 25,000 clinical psychologists.

• **Counseling psychology.** This specialization focuses on normal people who are having difficulty coping with personal conflicts. The counseling psychologist uses some of the same techniques as the clinical psychologist to help clients face their anxieties, emotional difficulties, or interpersonal conflicts.

• **Developmental psychology.** This specialization focuses on the study of behavioral changes that occur at different stages of life. Developmental psychologists attempt to define, measure, and explain different types of behavior that occur from birth to death. Areas such as vocational and emotional development require that the developmental psychologist explain behaviors that almost all humans experience as well as individual differences that occur in the development process. By doing so, the developmental psychologist helps define abnormal changes in development.

• **Social psychology.** This specialization focuses on how humans are affected by the environment in which they live. Social psychologists study the ways in which people interact with one another and with their environment. They study the influences of the family, school, or work setting on the behavior of individuals.

• **Experimental psychology.** This specialization focuses on scientific experiments on particular aspects of behavior. These studies can be conducted to determine animal or human behavior. The results of these studies can help explain such things as motivation for behavior or steps in the learning process. This is the largest specialization within the field of psychology.

• **Psychometry.** This specialization focuses on the measurement of intelligence, personality, and aptitude. Psychometrists use an array of tests to develop a profile of a client or patient for the clinical or counseling professional. They are knowledgeable in the areas of test construction, test administration, and test interpretation.

• **School psychology.** This specialization focuses on both diagnostic and remedial work with a range of children in the public and private school setting. School psychologists can be involved in diagnosing such things as learning disabilities and gifted and talented students. They work with parents, teachers, and children to facilitate the educational success of children.

• **Educational psychology.** This specialization focuses on the way children and adults learn. Unlike the school psychologist, who can diagnose and treat a learning problem, the educational psychologist studies the learning process from a scholarly perspective.

• **Industrial psychology.** This specialization focuses on the relationship between employees and their work environments. Industrial psychologists study such things as work and motivation, job satisfaction, productivity, and ergonomics. They advise management on changes in the work environment that will improve productivity, morale, and satisfaction.

• **Engineering psychology.** This specialization focuses on the design of engineering systems where people interact with machines. Engineering psychologists not only contribute to increased productivity but also to increased worker safety. Often, engineering psychologists develop teaching aids to help train workers to operate and use new equipment in a safe and effective manner.

• **Forensic psychology.** People in this specialization apply their knowledge of psychology to the legal field. For example, they might work with inmates with emotional and mental problems or work with the courts on child custody issues. They also might evaluate a person's competence to stand trial or consult on jury selection or eyewitness testimony.

Like other occupations within the field of rehabilitation services, psychologists who work in the clinical and counseling areas of the profession can work with all types of people. However, clinical and counseling psychologists often specialize in and treat only certain groups of people. For example, some psychologists treat children, while others specialize in treating college students, working adults, women, or the elderly.

Psychologists can also specialize in the types of mental disorders they treat. For example, some might treat people who are suffering from depression. Others might treat people with bipolar disorder, schizophrenics, or people with personality disorders.

As mentioned earlier, many psychologists teach and do research within a college or university setting. Those who work in an academic setting work with colleagues and graduate students in conducting their research. Many teach undergraduate and graduate courses. However, the primary group of people with whom these psychologists interact is other professionals. By publishing and speaking about their research findings, this group of psychologists expands the basic knowledge of the field.

Where Psychologists Work

While the popular image of the psychologist's workplace is an office where therapy sessions take place, the fact is that most psychologists work in colleges and universities. This is partially attributed to the fact that more than 60 percent of psychologists hold Ph.D.s. Interestingly, more psychologists are involved in teaching and research today than are involved in clinical practice.

Nonetheless, psychologists do work in private clinical practices and in hospital settings. They are employed in public and private mental hospitals as well as in the psychiatric units of comprehensive hospitals. Psychologists are employed in group homes and halfway houses. Some work for government agencies; others do consulting for business and industry.

How to Qualify to Become a Psychologist

Because the opportunities for people with only a bachelor's or master's degree are quite limited, a doctorate in psychology is highly recommended. For those planning to go on to graduate school in psychology, an undergraduate degree in psychology is excellent preparation. Upon completion of the undergraduate degree, students can be admitted directly into some Ph.D. programs.

Some universities that do research in psychology might offer an entering Ph.D. student a graduate fellowship or assistantship, which pays for tuition and fees and provides a monthly living stipend while completing doctoral studies. These graduate fellowships and assistantships go to the best students applying for entry into the program. Therefore, it is important to do well in the undergraduate program and gain related experience through internships, practicums, or cooperative education.

Completion of a graduate program approved by the American Psychological Association (APA) is important. Many positions, particularly university teaching and counseling positions, require a degree from an APA-accredited institution.

What Can You Earn as a Psychologist?

Psychologists with advanced degrees and entering their first year of work had a median annual salary of $48,500 in the 2007 PayScale.com survey. For those with five to nine years of experience and advanced degrees, the median annual salary was $61,500.

Like other social and rehabilitation specialties, the setting in which psychologists work can make a difference in their median annual salary. The following list shows the median pay for psychologists in various settings.

Nonprofit organizations	$58,500
Schools and colleges	$58,500
State and local government agencies	$58,700
Hospitals	$61,000
Federal government agencies	$63,000
Private practice	$61,700

How to Advance in Your Career as a Psychologist

While the career outlook for people with a bachelor's or master's degree in psychology continues to be competitive, the demand for psychologists with a Ph.D. is excellent. Therefore, advancement within the field of psychology is challenging for those who do not have at least a graduate degree. Those with a bachelor's in psychology can successfully pursue a professional career as a psychology aide or outside of psychology in areas that require a good understanding of human nature. An example might be a position in human resources in business and industry. However, within the field of psychology, the opportunities are extremely limited for those holding only a bachelor's degree.

This holds true even for those with a master's degree in psychology. The master's degree qualifies a person for assistant positions to Ph.D. psychologists involved in research, administration, or counseling.

Psychologists who hold Ph.D.s and are employed on the faculty of colleges and universities can advance through a system called tenure and promotion. After a certain number of years teaching and doing research, college and university faculty have their teaching and research reviewed by other faculty in their department, then their school, and then their university. After the review, the faculty member might be given tenure. This means that he or she can continue to do research and teach at that institution for the remainder of his or her professional life. There is also a promotion from assistant professor to associate professor. Later in an academic career, a faculty member can request another review for promotion to full professor—the highest level attainable.

Psychologists who are in the clinical or counseling areas have somewhat the same process of advancement described for rehabilitation counselors and social workers. Those who become certified and licensed can enter private practice. Those who work within hospitals and agencies can advance to supervisory and then administrative positions. They also have the option to move from smaller agencies to larger ones, with increasing amounts of responsibility for caseload and/or management.

Additional Sources of Information

American Association of State Psychology Boards
P.O. Box 4389
Montgomery, AL 36103

American Board of Professional Psychology
300 Drayton St., 3rd Floor
Savannah, GA 31401
abpp.org

American Board of Rehabilitation Psychology
750 First St. NE, Suite 100
Washington, DC 20002
http://abrp.org

American Psychoanalytic Association
309 E. 49th St.
New York, NY 10017
apsa.org

American Psychological Association
750 First St. NE, Suite 100
Washington, DC 20002
apa.org

Association of Black Psychologists
P.O. Box 55999
Washington, DC 20040-5999
abpsi.org

Association of Psychologists of Nova Scotia
1657 Barrington St., Suite 417
Halifax, NS B3J 2A1
Canada
apns.ca

British Columbia Psychological Association
1755 W. Broadway, Suite 202
Vancouver, BC V6J 4S5
Canada
psychologists.bc.ca

Canadian Psychological Association
141 Laurier Ave. W., Suite 702
Ottawa, ON K1P 5J3
Canada
cpa.ca/home

Council of Specialties in Professional Psychology
750 First St. NE
Washington, DC 20002-4242
cospp.org/acronyms.php

Manitoba Psychological Services, Inc.
FW208-CSB, 820 Sherbrook St.
Winnipeg, MB R3A 1R9
Canada
mps.mb.ca

National Association of School Psychologists
4340 East West Hwy., Suite 402
Bethesda, MD 20814
naspweb.org

Ontario Psychological Association
730 Yonge St., Suite 221
Toronto, ON M4Y 2B7
Canada
psych.on.ca

Ordre des Psychologues du Québec
1100 Avenue Beaumont, Bureau 510
Mont-Royal, QU H3P 3E5
Canada
ordrepsy.qc.ca/opqv2/fra/index.asp

Psychologists' Association of Alberta
520 Metropolitan Place
10303 Jasper Ave.
Edmonton, AB T5J 3N6
Canada
psychologistsassociation.ab.ca

MEDICAL SERVICES

One of the fastest growing segments of our economy is the medical profession. Often it is assumed that this simply means a demand for more doctors and nurses. However, the medical profession offers a broader array of career possibilities than that. In fact, one of the fastest growing areas in the medical field is medical rehabilitation.

There are four trends that are creating an increasing demand for people in rehabilitation services occupations related to medical services.

1. Managed care has become the predominant method whereby people receive medical services. Medical workers other than doctors follow cases and determine the level and duration of health care to be provided. Increasingly, health maintenance organizations (HMOs) and other insurance providers employ nurses, therapists, and counselors to form patient health-care teams.

2. The baby boomers, people born between 1946 and 1966, are aging. That means a larger percentage of our population will soon be categorized as elderly. They will require more health care. As people experience diminished capacity due to injury, illness, or simply the aging process, there will be a greater need for medical professionals to help them cope and compensate.

3. New technology is improving the quality of health care. As a result, there is a higher survival rate among those who are sick or injured. This

means that these patients will need assistance in recovering from or coping with their medical conditions.

4. There is a new emphasis on preventive care and nutritional services. Our society has become more health-conscious. People seek out fitness and nutrition experts to maintain their physical and mental well-being.

These phenomena combine to create more opportunities and diversity among the career options in rehabilitation services. From traditional psychiatrist to dietitian and nutritionist, the occupations in this group represent the blending of medicine, psychology, science, and technology to improve the quality of life.

PSYCHIATRIST

Psychiatry is one of the oldest medical specialties. Advances in brain imaging and pharmaceuticals have provided psychiatrists with new tools and techniques for the diagnosis and treatment of mental illnesses, making this an exciting career field if you are interested in pursuing a medical degree and working with people who have mental disorders.

The Work of Psychiatrists

A psychiatrist is a physician specializing in the prevention, diagnosis, and treatment of mental, addictive, and emotional disorders such as schizophrenia and other psychotic disorders, mood disorders, anxiety disorders, substance-related disorders, sexual and gender identity disorders, and adjustment disorders. Because of their medical education, psychiatrists understand the biological as well as the psychological and sociological components of illness. They are uniquely qualified to treat the whole person. Psychiatrists can order diagnostic tests, prescribe medications, evaluate and treat psychological and interpersonal problems, and intervene with families who are coping with stress, crises, and other problems.

Unlike the psychologist, psychiatrists examine patients following standard medical procedures. They first determine the person's physical condition and then use a systematic approach to gather the person's medical and mental histories. Often family histories become an important part of determining the nature and extent of the mental disorder.

After diagnosing the problem, psychiatrists formulate a treatment plan. This can involve other members of the medical team such as nurses, therapists, social workers, and counselors. It can also involve family members, coworkers, or court-appointed officials.

To treat their patients, psychiatrists use therapies such as psychotherapy, group therapy, and medications. Many times they will use a combination of these therapies.

Psychotherapy is the most widely used technique among psychiatrists. It involves the patient talking to the psychiatrist about his or her problem. During this process the psychiatrist asks the patient to explore feelings and insights in more detail. By helping patients explore their feelings, psychotherapy helps them arrive at a personal understanding of the root cause of their problem. It takes years of training to become proficient in this powerful technique.

While some psychiatrists teach and do research in medical schools as well as colleges and universities, most work in clinical settings. And like psychologists who work in these settings, psychiatrists work with all types of people who have mental, emotional, and behavioral disorders.

Like psychologists, psychiatrists often specialize and treat only certain types of people or disorders. Psychiatrists can treat such groups and conditions as abused children, emotionally disturbed teenagers, professional people under high stress, trauma victims, and others. They may also specialize in treating mental and emotional disorders or antisocial behavior.

Where Psychiatrists Work

Because of the diverse nature of their work, psychiatrists can be employed in a variety of settings. They can work with groups of other mental health professionals or in their own private practice. Psychiatrists work in the public and private sector, as well as in government agencies such as the Veterans Administration. Many psychiatrists are in private practice. Sometimes the private practice can include other rehabilitation services professionals such as counselors, social workers, or specialized therapists. To be able to admit their patients, when necessary, psychiatrists in private practice are also affiliated with a hospital.

Some psychiatrists are exclusively staff doctors at either private or public hospitals. A smaller number of psychiatrists work for community or government agencies. Some specialties within psychiatry such as industrial psychiatrists or forensic psychiatrists work in settings such as business and industry or the courts and correctional institutions.

How to Qualify to Become a Psychiatrist

If you are in high school and planning to become a psychiatrist, you should take a rigorous college preparatory curriculum including English, languages, humanities, social studies, mathematics, biology, chemistry, and physics.

The education of psychiatrists is long and requires a college degree followed by medical school, a residency program, and fellowship training.

- **Undergraduate education.** Four years at a college or university to earn a B.S. or B.A. degree, usually with a strong emphasis on basic sciences, such as biology, chemistry, and physics. Some students enter medical school with majors other than one of the sciences, but they have taken advanced science courses as their electives. Some enter medical school with a degree in engineering, which requires more math and science than a liberal arts degree, but they still need to make sure they have taken upper-level biology and chemistry courses in order to get into medical school.

- **Medical school.** Four years of medical education at one of the U.S. accredited medical schools (lcme.org) consists of preclinical and clinical parts. During the fourth year of medical school, if you want to specialize in psychiatry, you are able to take one or two elective courses related to this specialization. For example, if you have an interest in child psychiatry, you might take a course in general pediatrics or pediatric neurology. After completing medical school, you will complete more extensive training in psychiatry before being able to practice on your own.

- **Residency.** The residency program in psychiatry takes four years. It involves professional training under the supervision of senior psychiatry educators. After completing their residency training, most psychiatrists take an examination given by the American Board of Psychiatry and Neurology (abpn.com) to become a board certified psychiatrist.

• **Fellowship.** Psychiatry has a number of subspecialties, including the following:

- Child and adolescent psychiatry
- Geriatric psychiatry
- Forensic (legal) psychiatry
- Administrative psychiatry
- Alcohol and substance abuser psychiatry
- Emergency psychiatry
- Psychiatry in general medical settings (called consultation/liaison psychiatry)
- Mental retardation psychiatry
- Community psychiatry and public health
- Military psychiatry
- Psychiatric research

Most of these subspecialties require a one-year fellowship following the four-year residency in general psychiatry. There is one exception. Child and adolescent psychiatry requires two years of additional study.

In addition to fellowships, some people who are preparing to become psychiatrists choose additional training in psychoanalysis at special psychoanalytic institutes (naap.org/institutes.php). When the fellowship in psychiatry is completed, a certificate of added qualification is awarded.

What Can You Earn as a Psychiatrist?

After completing medical school, internships, residencies, and fellowships in psychiatry, the median starting salary for a psychiatrist with one year or less of work experience was $115,000, according to the 2007 PayScale.com survey. This means that half of the psychiatrists with this amount of experience made more than $115,000 and half made less. For psychiatrists with five to nine years of experience, the median salary was $136,000.

Salaries can vary depending on the setting in which psychiatrists are employed. For example, the median annual salary for those working in psychiatric hospitals is $130,500. In private practice, the median annual salary is $103,000. Psychiatrists who work for state and local governments have a median annual salary of $136,800, while those who work for the federal government have median annual salaries of $131,000.

How to Advance as a Psychiatrist

Future prospects for the field of psychiatry are excellent. There is a great need for psychiatrists in all aspects of public and private care. For psychiatrists in private practice, advancement comes in the form of professional recognition in the field and a sizable practice in an area of specialization. Prestige and status in the community contribute to wider recognition of the accomplishments of these professionals.

For those psychiatrists who practice on the staff of a hospital or agency, the opportunities for advancement are similar to other professionals in the field of rehabilitation services. They can be promoted to supervisory and administrative positions, and they can move to larger hospitals and agencies. Some may be asked to join the teaching faculty of medical schools.

Additional Sources of Information

An online directory of accredited medical schools is available from the Liaison Committee on Medical Education at lcme.org/directry.htm.

American Board of Psychiatry and Neurology
500 Lake Cook Rd., Suite 335
Deerfield, IL 60015
abpn.com

American Psychiatric Association
1000 Wilson Blvd., Suite 1825
Arlington, VA 22209-3901
psych.org

Canadian Psychiatric Association (CPA)
141 Laurier Ave. W., Suite 701
Ottawa, ON K1P 5J3
Canada
http://ww1.cpa-apc.org:8080/index.asp

National Association for the Advancement of Psychoanalysis
80 Eighth Ave., Suite 1501
New York, NY 10011
naap.org

PSYCHIATRIC AND MENTAL HEALTH NURSE

In the medical field, psychiatric nurses and mental health nurses are
important members of the treatment team. This is a nursing specialty that
cares for people with mental illness, and the emphasis is on developing
therapeutic relationships to address the needs of the whole person.

The Work of Psychiatric and Mental Health Nurses

Psychiatric and mental health nurses not only use traditional nursing
approaches but also develop therapeutic relationships with their patients
in order to engage them in the treatment process and effect change. To
accomplish this, psychiatric and mental health nurses must interact with
patients in a positive and collaborative manner, even when the patient is
not being cooperative.

The work of psychiatric and mental health nurses can be challenging.
Their patients have often been admitted to a psychiatric hospital or treatment center against their will. Therefore, psychiatric and mental health
nurses must develop skills in the following areas:

Assessment and diagnosis of patient conditions
Management of care
Symptom management and behavior change

Collaboration with families and other medical and rehabilitation
   practitioners
Evaluation of outcomes
Advocacy for patients and their families
Partnering with other communities

In addition to these professional skills, psychiatric and mental health nurses must have a great deal of patience.

Psychiatric and mental health nurses provide a broad range of psychiatric and medical services, depending on the level of education they have completed. For example, *psychiatric nursing aides* work under the supervision of nursing and medical staff. They answer patients' call lights; deliver messages; serve meals; make beds; and assist patients with eating, dressing, and bathing. They also take and record the patient's temperature, blood pressure, pulse rate, and respiration rate. They assist patients in getting in and out of bed and escort them to examining rooms. Aides play an important role in observing the patients' physical, mental, and emotional conditions and reporting changes to the nursing or medical staff.

Licensed practical nurses (LPNs) in the psychiatric and mental health field have one year of formal training. As a result, they are qualified to prepare and give injections, apply dressings, and monitor patients. They can also collect samples for testing and can perform routine lab tests. In some states, LPNs can administer prescribed medicines or start intravenous fluids.

Their work can range from doing intake work and assisting registered nurses (RNs) to assessing and treating psychiatric patients. With advanced degrees and extensive experience, psychiatric and mental health nurses can also do case management and psychotherapy. In some states, some psychiatric nurses can prescribe and monitor medication.

Registered nurses (RNs) treat patients with personality and mood disorders. They record patients' medical histories and symptoms, help to perform diagnostic tests and analyze results, operate medical equipment, administer treatment and medications, and help patients and their families with follow-up and rehabilitation. RNs with advanced degrees might have few or no direct patient care duties. They might work as case managers to ensure that medical needs of numerous patients are being met.

Where Psychiatric and Mental Health Nurses Work

Psychiatric and mental health nurses address the health-care needs of individuals who have psychiatric disorders, substance use problems, or medical conditions from injury or disability. They can also work with the patient's family members.

Psychiatric and mental health nurses work in psychiatric hospitals, treatment centers, physician offices, nursing homes, assisted living facilities, and other mental health settings. Some nurses work on the business side of health care and manage treatment units and facilities. Other employers of psychiatric and mental health nurses who work on the business side include insurance companies, pharmaceutical manufacturers, and managed care organizations. Nurses with advanced degrees can teach on college and university faculties and conduct research.

How to Qualify to Become a Psychiatric or Mental Health Nurse

To become an LPN, you must complete one year of training at a state-approved vocational or technical school. LPN programs include both classroom study and supervised patient care. Once you have completed the program, you must pass a licensing examination, known as the NCLEX-PN, to become an LPN.

There are three educational paths to becoming an RN.

A bachelor's degree
An associate degree
A diploma from an approved nursing program

During your education to become a registered psychiatric and mental health nurse, you will take the same courses as other nursing students and, in addition, you will receive training in behavioral issues, psychiatric medication, and a variety of different therapies.

After receiving an RN degree, some psychiatric and mental health nurses pursue master's (M.S.N. or A.P.R.N.) and doctoral degrees (D.N.Sc., Ph.D.). These advanced degrees qualify you to hold supervisory and administrative positions, as well as to provide higher levels of patient care.

Some people first complete the LPN or receive a nursing diploma and take a position on a nursing staff and then use tuition reimbursement benefits to pursue their bachelor's degree in an RN-to-B.S.N. program. There are over six hundred RN-to-B.S.N. programs in the United States. Accelerated master's degree programs in nursing also are available. These programs combine one year of an accelerated B.S.N. program with two years of graduate study. The American Psychiatric Nursing Association (APNA) provides a link to graduate programs in psychiatric nursing http://apna .org/i4a/pages/index.cfm/pageid=3311.

What Can You Earn as a Psychiatric or Mental Health Nurse?

Psychiatric nurses with an RN degree and one year of experience had a median annual salary of $44,000 in 2007, according to PayScale.com. For those with five to nine years of experience, the median annual salary was $54,500.

Mental health nurses with an RN degree and one year of experience had a median annual salary of $35,000, and with five to nine years of experience, the median salary was $46,500.

With nursing specialties, the setting in which you work can make a difference in the median annual salary earned. Hospitals paid a median annual salary of $56,500 for psychiatric nurses and $46,000 for mental health nurses. Nonprofit organizations paid a median annual salary of $52,500 for psychiatric nurses and $43,500 for mental health nurses. State and local government agencies paid a median annual salary of $54,000 for psychiatric nurses and $46,800 for mental health nurses.

How to Advance in Your Career as a Psychiatric or Mental Health Nurse

As stated previously, some RNs start as LPNs or nursing aides and then go back to school to receive their RN or B.S.N. degree. Because of the demand for good psychiatric and mental health nurses with experience and good performance, promotions to more responsible positions are not uncommon.

Once in management, nurses can advance to assistant head nurse or head nurse and from there to assistant director, director, and vice president. Increasingly, management-level nursing positions require a graduate or an advanced degree in nursing or health services administration.

Additional Sources of Information

American Psychiatric Nurses Association
1555 Wilson Blvd., Suite 602
Arlington, VA 22209
apna.org

Canadian Nurses Association
50 Driveway
Ottawa, ON K2P 1E2
Canada
cna-nurses.ca

International Society of Psychiatric–Mental Health Nurses
2810 Crossroads Dr., Suite 3800
Madison, WI 53718
ispn-psych.org

National Alliance on Mental Illness
Colonial Place Three
2107 Wilson Blvd., Suite 300
Arlington, VA 22201-3042
nami.org

PROSTHETIST AND ORTHOTIST

Of the thousands of professionals in the field of rehabilitation services, there is one small group of specially trained professionals whose goal it is to improve the quality of life for those who suffer from debilitating conditions and loss of limbs. These are the prosthetists and orthotists. There are fewer than 2,500 of them in the United States, but their work is vitally important to the patients and doctors they serve.

Prosthetics and orthotics is the evaluation, fabrication, and custom fitting of artificial limbs and orthopedic braces. The American Academy of Orthotists and Prosthetists (oandp.org) defines the various positions in this field as follows:

Prosthetists provide patients with artificial limbs.

Orthotists provide patients with braces.

O&P assistants fabricate, repair, and maintain devices to provide maximum fit, function, and attractiveness.

Orthotic fitters participate in the fitting and delivery of premade devices.

O&P technicians fabricate and repair artificial limbs, braces, and devices according to a physician's prescription. They don't provide direct patient care.

The Work of Prosthetists and Orthotists

Professionals in the areas of prosthetics and orthotics become involved in the design, production, and fitting of devices that assist people with disabilities to simulate normal functions. Prosthetists design, make, and fit special devices for patients who have experienced total or partial loss of a limb. The devices they make are referred to as prosthetic devices.

While prosthetics date back to the days of wooden legs, today's prosthetic devices are made of advanced plastics and graphite composites. Gone are the immovable artificial limbs. Advances in this field have led to a number of components, including the foot, the ankle, knee controls, sockets, support systems, and skinlike coverings. In addition, mechanical switches, harnesses, or electric signals control the modern prosthetic device.

These advances in the field give the patient lightweight, durable, aesthetically pleasing replacement limbs. A good prosthetist must be well trained and knowledgeable about the newest developments in the prosthetic field.

Orthotists design and make braces, irons, stays, and splints, otherwise known as orthoses, for patients who suffer from disabling conditions resulting from accidents, disease, or congenital problems. The devices designed by orthotists provide needed support to the affected parts of the body.

Because orthotists treat a wide range of problems, most of their work requires that they custom fit devices for patients. This process includes interaction with the patient to prepare castings or impressions for the orthotic device. As a member of the patient's rehabilitation team, the orthotist continues to follow up with the patient after the device is fitted.

Prosthetists and orthotists work as part of a rehabilitation team of doctors, nurses, and therapists. Because they are involved in making the devices, these professionals also interact with business and industries that supply the materials and equipment to produce prosthetic and orthotic devices. It is not uncommon for prosthetists and orthotists to collaborate with materials engineers, biomedical engineers, mechanical engineers, or electrical engineers in the design and development of new devices.

Most important, they work directly with patients to present choices about different devices. They also help patients make decisions about the most appropriate design to fit their lifestyle and health condition.

Prosthetists typically work with accident victims and victims of diseases such as diabetes and cancer. They also work with children and the elderly. Generally, the prosthetist first sees a patient approximately six weeks after surgery. At that point, the patient is fitted for a preparatory prosthesis. The permanent prosthesis is usually prepared and fitted several months later, depending on the individual's recovery rate. Periodic checkups help ensure a good fit, so prosthetists develop long-term professional relationships with their patients.

Orthotists' patients include victims of such conditions as cerebral palsy, spina bifida, hemophilia, spinal cord injuries, brain damage, stroke, muscular dystrophy, arthritis, and multiple sclerosis. Orthotists typically work with a qualified technician to make the appropriate device for each patient.

Like the prosthetist, the orthotist is a member of the patient's rehabilitation team. Depending on the condition, the orthotist may develop a long-term professional relationship with some patients. However, because the orthotist also treats victims with minor injuries from accidents or sporting events, the relationship with patients can be short-term as well.

Like so many professionals in the field of rehabilitation services, prosthetists and orthotists often specialize either in certain groups of people or in particular types of disabilities. Specialization limits the people with whom the prosthetist and orthotist work. For example, some may only work with athletes and orthopedic doctors. Others can work exclusively with cancer patients and oncologists. The options are almost limitless.

Where Prosthetists and Orthotists Work

Prosthetists and orthotists work in diverse settings. They can be employed by health-care industries involved in the manufacture of prosthetic and orthotic devices. They can also work in privately owned facilities or laboratories. There are more than 1,500 such member companies in the American Orthotic and Prosthetic Association.

Some hospitals and specialized medical facilities also employ prosthetists and orthotists on staff. However, almost all prosthetists and orthotists see patients in the hospital. They often must examine patients after surgery or an accident to begin the process of fitting them for a device. They may also see patients in the hospital again if the device needs to be altered due to changing health conditions.

How to Qualify to Become a Prosthetist or an Orthotist

While some people prepare for this field with a bachelor's degree in engineering or science, others obtain an undergraduate degree in prosthetics or orthotics from one of the board-approved programs at colleges and universities in the United States. Those who obtain a degree in another discipline can complete postgraduate course work in prosthetics and/or orthotics. To be certified, a person needs an additional year of clinical experience if his or her undergraduate degree is in prosthetics or orthotics. If the undergraduate degree is in another area, one to two additional years of clinical experience can be required for certification.

This field requires certification by the American Board for Certification in Orthotics and Prosthetics. While the number of certified orthotists is only slightly larger than the number of certified prosthetists, almost one-third of all people certified by the board are certified in both fields.

Continuing education is imperative in this field. It is important to know that prosthetists and orthotists cannot maintain their certification without continued education. In the United States, there are eight educational programs that prepare O&P practitioners to become certified by the American Board for Certification in Orthotics and Prosthetics (ABC), listed at abcop .org. Three are bachelor's-level degree programs and five are master's or postbaccalaureate certificate programs. Each program is accredited by the Commission on Accreditation for Allied Health Education (CAAHEP), the national accreditation agency for the orthotics and prosthetics profession. Programs are offered by the following schools:

California State University Dominguez Hills (CSUDH) (baccalaureate and certificate)—Aliso Viejo, CA

Century College (certificate)—White Bear Lake, MN

Georgia Institute of Technology (masters)—Atlanta, GA

Newington Certificate Program in Orthotics and Prosthetics— Newington, CT

Northwestern University (certificate)—Chicago, IL

University of Texas Southwestern Medical Center (baccalaureate)— Dallas, TX

University of Washington (baccalaureate)—Seattle, WA

At this writing, two more programs are being developed at the following schools:

Eastern Michigan University (graduate certificate)—Ypsilanti, MI

St. Petersburg College (baccalaureate)—St. Petersburg, FL

O&P Assistant Programs

At this time, there is only one O&P assistant program, which is pursuing accreditation by the ABC. It is offered by Oklahoma State University–Okmulgee in Okmulgee, Oklahoma, and it provides students with fundamental knowledge and skills. It is accredited by the National Commission on Orthotic and Prosthetic Education (NCOPE).

ABC Registered Orthotic Fitter

There are five pathways to becoming an ABC registered orthotic fitter:

Pathway 1. Two years of orthotic fitter experience (minimum of 3,800 hours) under the supervision of an ABC certified practitioner.

Pathway 2. One year of orthotic fitter experience (minimum of 1,900 hours) under the supervision of an ABC certified practitioner in an ABC accredited patient care facility.

Pathway 3. Successful completion of an ABC approved orthotic fitter education program and 1,000 hours of orthotic fitter experience. The following are approved orthotic fitter educational seminars:

Trulife Healthcare
Trulife Education Department
Jackson, MI
camphealthcare.com/edu/ciat.html

DeRoyal
DeRoyal Industries, Inc.
Powell, TN
deroyal.com

The Medical Careers Institute at Coordinated Health's
    Orthotic Fitter Course
Bethlehem, PA
themedicalcareersinstitute.com

Surgical Appliance/Truform
Cincinnati, OH
surgicalappliance.com/training.html

Applied Technology Institute/SOP
Adrian, MI
sopcourses.org

Otto Bock
Minneapolis, MN
ottobock.com

Pathway 4. Possession of an orthotic fitter license issued by a state orthotic/prosthetic licensing board.

Pathway 5. Possession of an orthotic practitioner credential awarded by ABC or another national orthotic/prosthetic credentialing body.

O&P Technician Programs

There are four O&P technician programs accredited by the National Commission on Orthotic and Prosthetic Education (NCOPE). They offer associate degree and certificate programs and are offered by the following schools:

Baker College of Flint—Flint, MI
Century College—White Bear Lake, MN
Francis Tuttle—Oklahoma City, OK
Spokane Falls Community College—Spokane, WA

Additional information about O&P practitioner, assistant, and technician schools may be found at ncope.org.

What Can You Earn as a Prosthetist or Orthotist?

In 2007, the PayScale.com salary survey reported that the median salary for a licensed prosthetist or orthotist with one year or less of work experience was $44,400. This means that half of the prosthetists and orthotists participating in the salary survey made more than $44,400 and half made less. For prosthetists or orthotists with five to nine years of experience, the median salary was $47,500.

Depending on the setting in which prosthetists or orthotists work, salaries can vary. For example, the median annual salary for those working in private practice is $47,900, and in hospitals, it is $47,300. In companies, the median annual salary is $47,700.

How to Advance in Your Career as a Prosthetist or Orthotist

In the field of prosthetics and orthotics, there is a serious shortage of trained professionals. With the technological advances in this field and the increasing demand among the aging population and wounded soldiers, the demand for prosthetists and orthotists is excellent.

Certification and increasing amounts of experience assure prosthetists and orthotists that they will be able to advance in their field. Experienced prosthetists and orthotists supervise technicians in industry and laboratories. Like other rehabilitation services professionals, prosthetists and orthotists can move from small facilities and hospitals to larger ones. In these instances they generally take on more supervisory and administrative responsibility.

The Future Outlook for Prosthetists and Orthotists

Once your education and residency are successfully completed and you've received your certification, your job security is excellent and it is likely that a number of opportunities will be available to you. Future opportunities are related to the American Academy of Orthotists and Prosthetists statistics that over 150,000 people in the United States lose a limb annually and more than 1.5 million Americans have had amputations and need ongoing care. In addition, 54 million Americans experience functional limitations due to an impairment or health condition.

Countries that are at war or lack the facilities or personnel available in the industrialized world have many people who have lost limbs or experienced functional limitation due to disease or accident. Some prosthetists and orthotists work with or volunteer through international programs that assist these underserved populations. See Chapter 12, "International Humanitarian Work."

Additional Sources of Information

For more information or to request a career kit, you can e-mail careers@oandp.org.

American Academy of Orthotists and Prosthetists
526 King St., Suite 201
Alexandria, VA 22314
oandp.org

The American Board for Certification in Orthotics, Prosthetics, and
 Pedorthics (ABC)
330 John Carlyle St., Suite 210
Alexandria, VA 22314
apcop.org

American Orthotic and Prosthetic Association
330 John Carlyle St., Suite 200
Alexandria, VA 22314
aopanet.org

Canadian Association for Prosthetics and Orthotics
605-294 Portage Ave.
Winnipeg, MB R3C 0B9
Canada
pando.ca

National Commission on Orthotic and Prosthetic Education (NCOPE)
330 John Carlyle St., Suite 200
Alexandria, VA 22314
ncope.org

MEDICAL SOCIAL WORKER

Medical social workers are members of a unique group of social workers
who specialize in helping patients handle their medical problems. They
are an important part of health teams composed of physicians, nurses, and
therapists who develop treatment plans to help patients cope with injury
and chronic or terminal illness.

The Work of Medical Social Workers

Medical social workers can focus on the needs of injured, transplant, heart
attack, cancer, AIDS, or Alzheimer's patients. They gather medical data
about the patient and the circumstances in the patient's life that might
affect his or her medical condition. Some examples of the types of work

that medical social workers can do range from monitoring psychological and physiological reaction to treatment and medication to assisting a terminally ill patient in preparing a will.

In addition, the medical social worker can serve as the liaison among the doctors, the therapists, the patient, and the family. In fact, it is sometimes the medical social worker who has the responsibility of explaining the treatments and their purpose to the patient and the family. In some cases, the medical social worker, like the psychiatric social worker, serves as an ombudsman between the hospital and the patient and/or the family.

Medical social workers generally work with patients in public and private hospitals. Some medical social workers can specialize in working with certain types of illness or certain types of people. For example, a medical social worker can work exclusively with geriatric, hospice, or AIDS patients, or he or she can work with terminally ill children.

In general, medical social workers are members of a team including doctors, therapists, counselors, and nurses. Medical social workers generally work under the direct supervision of doctors.

Where Medical Social Workers Work

While some medical social workers work for the same government and community agencies or institutions as other social workers, most are employed by hospitals, nursing homes, hospice programs, and other medical facilities.

With home health care increasing, some medical social workers go into private practice. Often this is a group practice with a team of other health professionals dedicated to providing outpatient and home health care.

How to Qualify to Become a Medical Social Worker

Medical social workers must have a master's degree in social work with a specialization in medical social work. These studies include graduate courses in human growth and development, social welfare policies, and methods of social work. This specialization requires a heavy concentration of medically related course work.

All graduate students in social work are required to have at least one year of clinical experience in an agency, hospital, or school under the direct supervision of an experienced M.S.W. However, medical social work students must complete their clinical experience under the direct supervision of experienced medical social workers and doctors.

Like other social workers, medical social workers are eligible for membership in the Academy of Certified Social Workers after two years of supervised experience. Attaining certification and a state license qualifies medical social workers to enter private practice.

What Can You Earn as a Medical Social Worker?

Medical social workers with advanced degrees entering their first year of work had a median annual salary of $34,500 in the 2007 PayScale .com survey. For those with five to nine years of experience and advanced degrees, the median annual salary was $43,000.

Like other social work specialties, the setting in which medical social workers are employed can make a difference in their median annual salary. The following list shows the median pay for medical social workers in various settings.

Nonprofit organizations	$41,000
State and local government agencies	$35,900
Hospitals	$42,100
Federal government agencies	$46,200
Private practice	$51,800

How to Advance as a Medical Social Worker

Medical social work is a field that is expected to grow faster than average through 2014. As a result, there will be increased opportunities for medical social workers to advance to supervisory and director positions.

Those with the proper education and experience can be promoted to unit supervisors or program directors. They move from a small hospital or health-care facility to a larger one and assume more responsibilities. Those who complete a doctorate may decide to teach and conduct research in a university setting.

Additional Sources of Information

American Federation of State, County, and Municipal Employees
1625 L St. NW
Washington, DC 20036
afscme.org

Canadian Association of Social Workers
383 Parkdale Ave., Suite 402
Ottawa, ON K1Y 4R4
Canada
casw-acts.ca

Council on Social Work Education
1725 Duke St., Suite 500
Alexandria, VA 22314
cswe.org
This organization publishes a directory of accredited B.S.W. and M.S.W. programs.

National Association of Social Workers
750 First St. NE, Suite 700
Washington, DC 20002-4241
naswdc.org

DIETITIAN AND NUTRITIONIST

Today people are much more conscious of their diet. Even fast-food restaurants are providing nutritional information about the foods they serve. While most people tend to think about dietitians and nutritionists in hospital settings, these professionals are playing a more important role in the lives of healthy individuals as well.

The Work of Dietitians and Nutritionists

Dietitians and nutritionists are responsible for planning meals that are not only high in nutritional value but are also appropriate in content and texture to meet the needs of special populations. In addition, some dietitians and nutritionists purchase food, equipment, and supplies as well as prepare meals. Others may supervise a professional staff that has the responsibility for purchasing and preparing meals.

It is common for dietitians and nutritionists to be counselors and educators as well as food scientists. They instruct and advise individuals and groups in the proper diet to meet specific needs such as reducing calories, fat, cholesterol, and/or carbohydrates in the diet. Special physical or medical conditions can also require reeducation on how to eat. In these cases, the dietitian or nutritionist can prepare printed materials as well as lectures.

There are generally seven areas in which dietitians and nutritionists can specialize.

• **Administrative or management dietitians.** These people oversee the planning and operation of major food service systems. The responsibilities of this specialization include administration of personnel, design and implementation of training programs, planning food systems, and developing departmental budgets.

• **Chief dietitians.** These professionals perform all of the responsibilities of administrative or management dietitians; however, they are usually found in hospital settings and have the added responsibility of clinical management as well as food service management. Specifically, chief dietitians monitor and maintain the records on each patient's dietary needs and reactions.

• **Clinical or therapeutic dietitians.** They plan and supervise the preparation of diets to meet patient needs. In these cases, either the patient's condition or the attending physician requires a special diet as part of the recovery process. Clinical dietitians are part of the medical team and advise patients, families, doctors, medical staff, and hospital administration on patients' dietary needs.

• **Community dietitians.** These specialists counsel individuals and groups on proper nutrition. As a member of community health programs, the purpose of dietitians in this specialization is to maintain health and prevent disease in the local community.

• **Business dietitians.** They perform a range of functions for various businesses and industries. Sometimes they appear in the media on behalf of grocery store chains. Often they will advise consumers on how to shop for nutritional foods that are in season or that fit a tight budget. Many business dietitians work for the food or restaurant industries. They also work on new product development and sales.

• **Education dietitians.** Professionals in this area teach food science and nutrition as well as food service courses in colleges and universities. They may also teach in hospitals. Many write books and publish articles about food and nutrition.

• **Dietitian consultants.** These dieticians have private practices where they advise major industries on food science and nutrition issues. Some conduct seminars for other professionals, and still others work under contract with nursing homes, health department programs, and hospitals to provide diet and nutrition counseling to patients and clients. Athletic programs at the collegiate, Olympic, and professional levels also employ dietitians and nutritionists to tailor dietary plans to the fitness needs of athletes.

All types of people need the counseling and guidance of dietitians and nutritionists. While it is common to think of these professionals in hospital settings, the increasing concern for fitness has increased the demand for their expertise. Some of the groups that dietitians and nutritionists serve include schoolchildren, expectant mothers, the elderly, diabetics, heart attack patients, athletes, overweight individuals, people recovering from serious illnesses and injuries, people with severe allergies, and people with eating disorders.

Where Dietitians and Nutritionists Work

The largest number of dietitians and nutritionists are employed in public and private hospitals. However, many are also employed in community health programs. They also work in fitness centers, wellness clinics, health maintenance organizations (HMOs), doctor's offices, training camps for athletes, public and private school systems, and business and industry.

How to Qualify to Become a Dietitian or Nutritionist

Dietitians and nutritionists are trained in the science of food and nutrition. An undergraduate degree in foods and nutrition or food service management is a basic requirement for entering this field.

Typically these programs of study include courses in foods and nutrition, food service management, chemistry, bacteriology, physiology, mathematics, psychology, sociology, and economics. In addition, a one-year internship is required.

What Can You Earn as a Dietitian or Nutritionist?

Dietitians and nutritionists who are entering their first year of work had a median annual salary of $37,486 in the 2007 PayScale.com survey. For those with five to nine years of experience and advanced degrees, the median annual salary was $45,530.

The setting in which dietitians and nutritionists are employed can make a difference in their median annual salary. The following list shows the median pay for dietitians and nutritionists in various settings.

Nonprofit organizations	$41,500
State and local government agencies	$41,000
Hospitals	$43,000
Federal government agencies	$45,000
Companies	$43,700
Private practice	$44,000

How to Advance as a Dietitian or Nutritionist

According to the U.S. Bureau of Labor Statistics, the demand for dietitians and nutritionists is expected to grow faster than the average through 2014. The reason for this growth can be attributed to increased focus on disease prevention through proper eating. This will increase the demand for nutritional counseling in all aspects of our lives.

As the dietitian or nutritionist gains experience, he or she will often move from a salaried position to private practice. This trend is expected to increase as public agencies downsize their staff and contract for specialized services.

Other dietitians and nutritionists become directors and administrators at schools, hospitals, and health-care or government agencies. Like other rehabilitation services professionals, they sometimes move from small agencies and organizations to larger ones where they take on increasing amounts of responsibility. Those with advanced degrees teach and do research in colleges and universities.

Additional Sources of Information

American Dietetic Association
120 S. Riverside Plaza, Suite 2000
Chicago, IL 60606-6995
eatright.org

Dietitians of Canada
480 University Ave., Suite 604
Toronto, ON M5G 1V2
Canada
dietitians.ca

CHAPTER

8

THERAPEUTIC SERVICES

According to the U.S. Department of Labor, the occupations known as therapists are concerned with the treatment and rehabilitation of persons with mental, emotional, and physical disabilities. In their work, therapists develop or restore functions, prevent loss of physical capacities, and maintain optimum performance.

Therapists generally work in medically oriented institutions, schools or other community facilities, or in individual homes. The general focus for therapies is improving an individual's social, emotional, educational, occupational, daily living, and/or recreational skills. The strategies of therapists may include such means as exercise, creative arts, massage, heat, ultrasound, water, and other therapeutic activities. Generally, therapists require a physician's referral. Treatment strategies are planned and implemented by a team of professionals that includes not only therapists but also physicians, nurses, social workers, and counselors. Because of the teamwork-based nature of these professions, all therapists must be exceptionally competent in their record keeping. Every other member of the team relies on the therapist's input for diagnosis and treatment purposes. Therefore, the records must be accurate and up-to-date.

As a result of the aging of our population, new medical technology that increases the survival rates of critically ill patients, and increases in the practice of early discharge from hospitals, there is a growing need for all types of therapists. In addition, the enactment of the Americans with Disabilities Act has created a new demand for therapists, particularly occupational therapists, to help businesses and industry meet the requirements of the law.

PHYSICAL THERAPIST

Contributed by Diane U. Jette, PT, D.Sc.
Chairperson and Professor
Department of Rehabilitation and Movement Science
The University of Vermont

The Work of Physical Therapists

Physical therapists work with people to prevent injury; improve or restore function following disease, injury, or loss of limb; and prevent disability. To accomplish this, physical therapists examine patients, make a diagnosis of their movement-related problems, and develop a plan of care based on patients' individual needs.

The approach begins with a thorough examination of the patient that includes taking a health history, testing, and measuring the patient's overall physical condition. After gathering this data, the physical therapist prepares a plan of care and then administers an intervention.

Interventions can include such things as manual therapy, therapeutic exercises, application of physical agents, and massage. Therapeutic exercises are generally designed to improve and maintain muscle function, body alignment, balance, and endurance. The physical agents that these therapists can use include such things as heat, cold, sound waves, water, and electricity. Examples of these agents are whirlpool baths, hot and cold packs, ultrasound, and therapeutic pools. Massage and traction are sometimes administered to relieve pain.

Some physical therapists evaluate, fit, and adjust prosthetic devices for people with amputations and orthotic devices for people with certain types of paralysis or pain. They also recommend modifications to the devices to improve usefulness to the patient. In addition to conferring with prosthetists and orthotists, they also confer with physicians and other health practitioners involved in the rehabilitation of their patients.

Physical therapists instruct, motivate, and assist patients in exercises and other forms of treatment. They also instruct family members in the physical therapy procedures being used to rehabilitate the patient. They can also be responsible for orienting, instructing, and directing the work activities of physical therapy assistants and aides.

Some may plan and conduct lectures and seminars for medical and professional staff, physical therapy students, and/or community groups. Those with advanced education and experience can train and evaluate clinical students or conduct research and write technical articles and reports for publication.

Like many rehabilitation services occupations, physical therapists serve all types of people. However, like other professionals, experienced physical therapists often limit treatment to specific patient groups and/or disabilities. Some of these specialties include orthopedic physical therapy, pediatric physical therapy, cardiovascular-pulmonary physical therapy, neurological physical therapy, and geriatric physical therapy.

Where Physical Therapists Work

Many physical therapists work in hospitals and rehabilitation centers and in private practices owned by themselves or other physical therapists. However, physical therapists are also employed in schools, home health agencies, nursing homes, hospices, sports medicine centers, athletic departments of colleges and universities, and fitness programs in business and industry.

How to Qualify to Become a Physical Therapist

The basic educational requirement to enter the field of physical therapy is a post-baccalaureate degree in physical therapy. Most physical therapist educational programs award students the doctorate in physical therapy (D.P.T.) on graduation. A few programs still offer students the master's degree, either an M.S.P.T. or M.P.T. There are currently two hundred-ten institutions offering degrees across the country.

The course work required to qualify for entry into a physical therapy program includes biology, chemistry, physics, anatomy, physiology, psychology, and statistics. Once in an educational program, students take courses such as neuroanatomy, biomechanics, human growth and development, pharmacology, health policy, health promotion, health-care ethics, pathophysiology, physical therapy patient management, and research. Students must also complete at least thirty-two weeks of full-time supervised clinical experience.

Admission to physical therapy educational programs is highly competitive. Upon graduation from an accredited physical therapy program, physical therapists must pass a licensure examination.

During high school, the best preparation for a career in physical therapy is a strong background in physical and biological sciences. In addition, it is advisable to do volunteer work in a physical therapy setting.

For those who do not plan to pursue a graduate degree in physical therapy, a career in this area is still possible as a physical therapy assistant. Physical therapy assistants usually complete an associate degree and work under the direct supervision of a physical therapist. They carry out treatment plans, train patients in exercises and use of special equipment, and report patient progress. Licensure is also required for most physical therapy assistants.

What Can You Earn as a Physical Therapist?

According to Health Career Center (mshealthcareers.com/index.htm), the average annual salary for physical therapists is $64,800. The salary range for physical therapists was reported to be $51,900 to $82,700. Acquiring more education and experience will qualify you for the higher salary ranges.

How to Advance as a Physical Therapist

The aging of the population will have two significant impacts on the field of physical therapy. The first will be an increased demand for the services of physical therapists, and the second will be an increased number of retirements from the field. Increased activity in sports and other physical activities is also adding to the demand for physical therapists.

All of this means that after a few years of clinical practice, many physical therapists will probably seek additional certification as specialists. Specialty certifications include orthopedics, neurology, sports therapy, geriatrics, pediatrics, and cardiovascular-pulmonary therapy.

Experienced physical therapists can also become supervisors and directors in hospitals, skilled nursing facilities, home health agencies, and other types of clinics. Many physical therapists move from salaried positions to owning their own private practices. Many physical therapists also return to school to obtain a Ph.D. to allow them to teach and do research in colleges and universities.

Additional Sources of Information

American Physical Therapy Association

1111 N. Fairfax St.

Alexandria, VA 22314

apta.org

Canadian Physiotherapy Association (CPA)

2345 Yonge St., Suite 410

Toronto, ON M4P 2E5

Canada

physiotherapy.ca

OCCUPATIONAL THERAPIST

Contributed by Shelly J. Lane, Ph.D., OTR/L, FAOTA

Professor and Chair, Department of Occupational Therapy

Assistant Dean of Research, SAHP

Virginia Commonwealth University

The Work of Occupational Therapists

According to the American Occupational Therapy Association (AOTA, 2006), the goal of occupational therapy is to "help individuals achieve independence in all facets of their lives." Occupational therapists are an important part of an intervention team that works to help people with mental, physical, developmental, or emotional disabilities acquire, relearn, or develop compensatory approaches to accomplish day-to-day skills, engage in meaningful activity, achieve independence, and assist people in developing the "skills for the job of living."

By tailoring treatment programs to meet the unique needs of each client, the occupational therapist plays an important part in the development and implementation of an overall treatment plan. Some of the responsibilities of the occupational therapist include the following:

- Planning manual and creative arts activities to aid clients in restoration or adaptation of skills
- Helping clients practice prevocational, vocational, and homemaking skills for daily living

- Facilitating clients' participation in educational, recreational, and social activities designed to help them regain physical or mental functioning or adjust to handicaps
- Designing and constructing special equipment and suggesting adaptations to living arrangements to maximize personal independence

In addition, occupational therapists consult with other members of the team including doctors, nurses, teachers, physical and speech therapists, and social workers or counselors. They also conduct training seminars for patients, families, or other professionals. Some make and fit adaptive devices in consultation with prosthetists and orthotists.

Occupational therapists almost always work with individuals in special groups or with particular disabilities. According to the American Occupational Therapy Association (AOTA), occupational therapists significantly improve rehabilitation for many people with impairments due to arthritis, cancer, or other debilitating illnesses; head or spinal cord injuries; orthopedic, work, or sports-related injuries; amputation; burns; head trauma; stroke and other neurological conditions; mental illness; or developmental disabilities. Some occupational therapists evaluate the abilities and needs of children and recommend treatment and equipment adaptation to maximize their learning in a school environment. Others work with individuals with mental retardation or emotional disturbance. In addition, occupational therapists can work with individuals who have a history of substance abuse, or with people with eating disorders. Like so many occupations in rehabilitation services, the specialties within occupational therapy seem almost limitless.

The AOTA has identified emerging practice areas for occupational therapy. These include intervention roles in preventing or addressing school and youth violence, driver training and rehabilitation, low vision services, community health services, back-to-work services, and consultation roles in health and wellness and home/work modification.

Where Occupational Therapists Work

The largest percentage of occupational therapists work in traditional acute, rehabilitative, or psychiatric hospitals. The second-largest percentage work in public school settings, where they assist parents, teachers, and children in adapting and developing functional skills for daily living. Other settings where many occupational therapists work include nursing homes, home health-care agencies, clinics, community mental health agencies, consulting firms, and private practice.

How to Qualify to Become an Occupational Therapist

Entry into the profession is now at the master's level; there are some opportunities to enter with a clinical doctorate. Advanced educational opportunities may involve the clinical doctorate (O.T.D.), which emphasizes advanced clinical skills, leadership, or the research doctorate (Ph.D. or Sc.D.). At this level, the emphasis is on research and teaching. An entry-level occupational therapist must be certified by the National Board for Certification in Occupational Therapy. This requires passing the certification examination after completion of an entry-level masters or clinical doctoral degree from an accredited occupational therapy program.

Prerequisite course work for entrance into occupational therapy programs includes a background in basic and applied sciences. While the specific course requirements vary between programs, generally you will be required to take courses in biology, chemistry, physiology, anatomy, neurology, psychology, and sociology. Course work within the program also will include human anatomy and neuroanatomy; the application of basic science to disabilities and medical conditions; occupational therapy theory, assessment, and intervention; activity analysis and application; statistics; research; and the ethics of the profession. Other course work may be required specific to individual programs. All accredited programs of occupational therapy require at least a six-month clinical internship. However, some will require more than that. In the United States, there are more than three-hundred accredited programs in occupational therapy.

Occupational therapy is a regulated practice. In the United States, forty-three states require licensure in addition to passing the national certification examination; other states continue to work toward licensure.

How to Advance as an Occupational Therapist

With the current increase in employment opportunities for occupational therapists, it is becoming increasingly competitive to enter this field. According to the U.S. Bureau of Labor Statistics, this field will grow faster than average between now and 2014.

Occupational therapists generally begin their careers as staff therapists, and after several years of experience they gain the status of senior therapist. Senior therapists may become involved in supervising occupational therapy students and volunteers in addition to assuming more administrative responsibilities. With additional training and education, therapists can move into teaching, research, and program director positions.

Additional Sources of Information

American Occupational Therapy Association
4720 Montgomery Ln.
P.O. Box 31220
Bethesda, MD 20824-1220
aota.org

Canadian Association of Occupational Therapists
CTTC Bldg., Suite 3400
1125 Colonel By Dr.
Ottawa, ON K1S 5R1
Canada
caot.ca

ART THERAPIST

While art therapy might sound like a new career field, it has been around for over sixty years. It emerged as a distinct profession in the 1940s when hospitals and rehabilitation facilities recognized that art therapy programs, used along with traditional therapies, helped people to express their emotions and enhanced the recovery process, health, and wellness. Today, art therapy is used not only to treat children and adults but also has grown into an effective and important method of assessing treatment needs.

Art therapy is used to treat a range of mental and emotional problems such as anxiety, depression, substance abuse, family relationship issues, abuse and domestic violence, and difficulties related to disability and illness, trauma, and loss. Art therapy has also been found to benefit stroke, cancer, burn, pain, postsurgical, HIV, and asthma patients. Currently the field of art therapy has gained attention in health-care facilities throughout the United States and within psychiatry, medicine, psychology, counseling, education, and the arts.

The American Art Therapy Association (AATA), the official member organization for professionals and students, was founded in 1969 to develop and promote educational, professional, and ethical standards for the field of art therapy. The AATA sponsors annual conferences, approves educational programs, and publishes *Art Therapy: Journal of the American Art Therapy Association* (first published in 1983), the quarterly *AATA Newsletter*, the *AATA E-Newsletter*, books, and monographs.

The Work of Art Therapists

According to the American Art Therapy Association, art therapy is a mental health profession that uses the creative process of art making to improve and enhance the physical, mental, and emotional well-being of individuals of all ages. It is based on the belief that the creative process of artistic self-expression helps people to resolve conflicts and problems, develop interpersonal skills, manage behavior, reduce stress, increase self-esteem and self-awareness, and achieve insight.

Art therapy integrates the fields of human development, visual art (drawing, painting, sculpture, and other art forms), and the creative process with models of counseling and psychotherapy.

Art therapists are unique members of a patient's rehabilitation team. After conferring with other members of the team to determine the nature of a patient's illness, the art therapist recommends a treatment plan and conducts programs to instruct the patient in art techniques. Both psychological knowledge and creative art skills are used.

Appraising the patient's various artistic statements can be an important part of the patient's recovery process. The progress and regression of each patient are reported to other members of the treatment team so that adjustments and adaptations can be made in the overall treatment plan.

According to the American Art Therapy Association, art therapy is an effective treatment for developmentally, medically, educationally, socially, or psychologically impaired persons. Most art therapists work with individuals, families, and groups. Like other rehabilitation services professionals, they may specialize in terms of groups of people and/or disabling conditions. Children and the elderly have been shown to benefit greatly from art therapy. This is particularly true when their ability to communicate has been inhibited by trauma, illness, or injury. In addition to their caseload, art therapists interact with a variety of medical and rehabilitation services professionals.

Where Art Therapists Work

There are fewer than one thousand art therapists in the country. Art therapists work in private offices, art rooms, or meeting rooms in facilities such as medical and psychiatric hospitals, outpatient facilities, residential treatment centers, halfway houses, shelters, schools, correctional facilities, elder-care facilities, pain clinics, universities, and art studios. The art therapist works as part of a team that includes physicians, psychologists, nurses, rehabilitation counselors, social workers, and teachers. Together, they determine and implement a client's therapeutic, school, or mental health program. Art therapists also work as primary therapists in private practice.

How to Qualify to Become an Art Therapist

Because the field of art therapy requires a strong understanding of the application of various art media and art processes to patient treatment, a master's degree and registration as an art therapist are required. There are over thirty AATA-approved master's degree programs and a growing number of undergraduate introductory courses and preparatory programs in art therapy. If you are planning to pursue a master's degree in art therapy, you should take four or five studio art courses and three or four psychology courses as part of your undergraduate work.

Applicants to art therapy master's degree programs must hold a bachelor's degree from an accredited college or university or have equivalent preparation from an institution outside the United States. In addition, they must submit a portfolio of original artwork and transcripts that document fifteen semester hours in studio art and twelve semester hours in psychology.

An AATA-approved art therapy master's degree program will be less than two years and must include a minimum of twenty-four graduate credit hours in the art therapy core curriculum.

Applicants to master's degree programs must hold a baccalaureate degree from an accredited U.S. institution or have equivalent academic preparation from an institution outside the United States. In addition, prospective students must submit a portfolio of original artwork and must document fifteen semester hours in studio art and twelve semester hours in psychology.

Educational requirements include courses in theories of art therapy, counseling, and psychotherapy; psychopathology; ethics and standards of practice; assessment and evaluation; individual, group, and family techniques; human and creative development; multicultural issues; research methods; and practicum experiences in clinical, community, and/or other settings.

Credentials

The Art Therapy Credentials Board (ATCB) Inc., an independent organization, grants the credential of Art Therapist Registered (ATR). To become a registered art therapist, you must submit documentation that you have completed an approved master's degree program and supervised postgraduate experience. Registered art therapists who successfully pass a written examination administered by the ATCB are qualified as Board Certified (ATR-BC). It is necessary to be recertified as a registered art therapist every five years. This is done by completing continuing education courses in which you earn approved continuing education credits (CECs). Recertification is important because it assures that you are keeping up-to-date with changes and advances in the field of art therapy.

What Can You Earn as an Art Therapist?

According to the AATA, earnings for art therapists vary depending on type of practice, job responsibilities, and practice location. In 2007, they report the average entry-level income is approximately $32,000 annually. Top salaries ranged between $50,000 and $80,000 for administrators and directors.

Art therapists with Ph.D.s and/or licensure to conduct a private practice in their state can earn an average of $85 to $120 per hour as private practitioners.

How to Advance as an Art Therapist

The demand for art therapists is expected to grow as the benefits of this type of therapy become more widely recognized. Because art therapists tend to work alone or as a member of a medically oriented team, the usual paths for advancement are not always possible. However, art therapists with advanced degrees can teach and do research. Others may write scholarly and technical publications to enhance their professional reputation. Those in private practice measure their advancement by the growth of their practice.

Additional Sources of Information

American Art Therapy Association (AATA), Inc.
5999 Stevenson Ave.
Alexandria, VA 22304
arttherapy.org

Art Therapy Credentials Board (ATCB), Inc.
3 Terrace Way, Suite B
Greensboro, NC 27403
atcb.org

Canadian Art Therapy Association
Box 538
Birtle, MB R0M 0C0
Canada
catainfo.ca

DANCE/MOVEMENT THERAPIST

Contributed by Jessica Young, LCPC, ADTR, GLCMA
President, Illinois Chapter of the American Dance Therapy
   Association and Faculty,
Dance/Movement Therapy and Counseling Department
Columbia College Chicago

The Work of Dance/Movement Therapists

Dance/movement therapy is a form of psychotherapy where the goal is to help clients achieve and maintain optimal well-being of body, mind, and spirit. Like art therapists, dance/movement therapists are often members of a team of experts involved in the client's care to ensure integrated services. They play an active role in assessing, treatment planning, implementing services, and discharge planning. Specifically, dance/movement therapists conduct a movement assessment to support a psychosocial assessment and body-based interventions to support goals on the treatment plan. The dance/movement therapist utilizes observational skills to note the movement qualities of the client and how they reflect presenting psychosocial issues and then creates movement interventions to facilitate physical and emotional shifts.

Appraising and facilitating each individual's self-expression through dance and movement is an important part of the recovery process. As for any therapist, the client's progress and regression are reported in detail to other members of the treatment team as indicators of change in the person's therapeutic process.

Dance/movement therapy has benefited many people across the life span, from infancy through older adulthood, addressing developmental milestones along the way. It is recognized as an important part of the treatment plan for people diagnosed with a variety of disorders including psychotic disorders, mood disorders, personality disorders, eating disorders, developmental disorders, learning disorders, and substance abuse. Dance/movement therapy is an effective modality for treating trauma as well as disruptions in early attachment, and the work of dance/movement therapists is being substantiated by current research in the field of neurobiology.

Dance/movement therapy is a small but growing field. As with other therapists, dance/movement therapists may develop specialized areas of interest such as working with trauma, eating disorders, or substance abuse, while others work with a wide variety of people. They also work within the context of prevention and with high-functioning individuals who are seeking enhanced personal growth.

Where Dance/Movement Therapists Work

Just over one thousand dance/movement therapists are credentialed in the United States. While psychiatric hospitals and long-term mental health organizations have tended to be the primary employers of dance therapists, the variety of settings employing dance/movement therapists is expanding. Dance/movement therapists are working in psychosocial day programs, veteran's hospitals, nursing homes and Alzheimer's programs, adult day-care facilities, drug treatment programs, public and private schools, prisons, youth residential programs, brain injury programs, and private practice.

Those in private practice have contracts with a number of health-oriented organizations. In these cases, dance/movement therapists provide therapy for the agencies' clients as well as their own private caseload.

How to Qualify to Become a Dance/Movement Therapist

Obviously, dance/movement therapists are trained in a variety of dance forms and body-based practices. In addition to a strong liberal arts background at the undergraduate level, dance therapists often take extensive course work in dance theory, improvisation, choreography, anatomy, kinesiology, and psychology at the undergraduate level. It is also important that dance/movement therapists have had experience in community and volunteer work. Many begin teaching dance and extend their experience to integrating dance into community-based services.

This undergraduate preparation is only the foundation. In the field of dance/movement therapy, the minimum degree requirement is a master's degree. Currently, five institutions offer master's degree programs approved by the American Dance Therapy Association.

In addition to approving graduate-level programs in dance/movement therapy, the American Dance Therapy Association also registers therapists who have met their criteria at two different levels. At the first level, dance/movement therapists are registered as being qualified to work as members of a treatment team in a clinical setting while receiving supervision. At the second level of registration, they are qualified to teach, supervise, and have a private practice.

What Can You Earn as a Dance/Movement Therapist?

According to Health Career Center (http://mshealthcareers.com/index .htm), the average salary for dance/movement therapists was $36,600 in 2007. The salary range for these professionals is $30,700 to $43,200. As previously stated, higher salaries are related to higher levels of education and experience.

How to Advance as a Dance/Movement Therapist

After receiving the second level of registration, and in many states full licensure as a counselor or therapist, some dance/movement therapists advance their professional development through directing and managing programs, teaching, supervising, and practicing privately. In addition, research in the field is both a need and an area of growth that can aid professional advancement. Other opportunities include presenting at conferences and workshops, writing scholarly and technical publications, and affiliating with professional organizations. While a master's degree is a terminal degree for dance/movement therapy, some go on to receive their Ph.D. in a related field such as psychology.

Additional Sources of Information

American Dance Therapy Association
2000 Century Plaza, Suite 108
10632 Little Patuxent Pkwy.
Columbia, MD 21044
adta.org

MUSIC THERAPIST

Contributed by Judy Simpson, MHP, MT-BC
Director of Government Relations, American Music
    Therapy Association

The Work of Music Therapists

Music therapists use music to address physical, emotional, cognitive, and social needs of individuals of all ages. After assessing the strengths and needs of each client, qualified music therapists develop a treatment plan with goals and objectives and then provide the indicated treatment. Music therapists structure the use of both instrumental and vocal music strategies to facilitate changes that are nonmusical in nature. Like other members of the rehabilitation team, music therapists collaborate with other professionals in providing interventions that meet the needs, capabilities, and interests of each patient.

These interventions can include the following:

Improvising or composing music with clients
Accompanying and conducting group music experiences
Providing instrument instruction

Directing music and movement activities

Structuring music listening opportunities

Music therapy interventions can be designed to facilitate movement, increase motivation, promote wellness, manage stress, alleviate pain, enhance memory, provide emotional support, create an outlet for expression, improve communication, and provide unique opportunities for interaction.

Music therapists work with children and adults with developmental disabilities, speech and hearing impairments, physical disabilities, psychiatric disorders, neurological impairments, and general medical illnesses, among others. Although music therapists work with over forty different patient populations, a significant number of music therapists provide services for persons with autism and other developmental and learning disabilities, Alzheimer's disease, mental health needs, medical illnesses, and physical disabilities.

Where Music Therapists Work

Music therapists work in many different settings including general and psychiatric hospitals, mental health agencies, physical rehabilitation centers, nursing homes, public and private schools, substance abuse programs, forensic facilities, hospice programs, and day-care facilities. Typically, full-time therapists work a standard forty-hour workweek. Some therapists prefer part-time work and choose to develop contracts with specific agencies, providing music therapy services for an hourly or contractual fee. In addition, a growing number of clinicians are choosing to start private practices in music therapy to benefit from opportunities provided through self-employment.

How to Qualify to Become a Music Therapist

Those who wish to become music therapists must earn a bachelor's degree or higher in music therapy from one of over seventy American Music Therapy Association (AMTA) approved colleges and universities. Course work involves three main areas: musical foundations, clinical foundations, and music therapy foundations and principles. Entry-level study also requires twelve-hundred hours of clinical training, including a supervised internship. Graduate programs in music therapy examine in more detail the clinical and professional issues important to music therapists and usually involve opportunities for conducting research.

Once the courses and clinical training are completed, students are eligible to take the national examination administered by the Certification Board for Music Therapists (CBMT), an independent, nonprofit certifying agency fully accredited by the National Commission for Certifying Agencies. After successful completion of the CBMT examination, graduates are issued the credential necessary to practice music therapy, Music Therapist–Board Certified (MT-BC). To demonstrate continued competence and to maintain this credential, music therapists are required to complete one hundred hours of continuing music therapy education or to retake and pass the CBMT examination within every five-year recertification cycle.

What Can You Earn as a Music Therapist?

In the field of creative arts therapy, music therapists have an average annual salary of $36,600, according to Health Careers Center (mshealthcareers .com/index.htm). The salary range for music therapists is $30,700 to $43,200. As in every social and rehabilitation services field, the more education and successful experience you have, the higher your salary.

How to Advance as a Music Therapist

Because hospitals are cutting back on the hiring of music therapists to save costs, opportunities in music therapy are expected to grow more slowly than average. However, there will be demands for music therapists in nursing care and assisted living facilities, as well as in psychological and rehabilitation facilities.

Advancement in the field of music therapy includes becoming a supervisor or director of a creative arts therapy department, activity therapy department, or rehabilitation therapy department. Some music therapists in private practice create music therapy agencies and hire other music therapists to provide more services.

Music therapists with advanced degrees and certification are qualified to teach at the university level. Music therapists at all levels of education write scholarly and technical publications to advance the field of music therapy.

As an increasing number of consumers seek noninvasive, alternative, and complementary therapies as treatment options, the need for music therapists continues to rise. An increased need for music therapists in early intervention programs, special education settings, geriatric facilities, and community-based services offers a variety of employment options. The next ten years hold positive opportunities for the music therapy profession.

Additional Sources of Information

American Music Therapy Association
8455 Colesville Rd., Suite 1000
Silver Spring, MD 20910
musictherapy.org

Canadian Association for Music Therapists
Wilfrid Laurier University
Waterloo, ON N2L 3C5
Canada
musictherapy.ca

Certification Board for Music Therapists
506 E. Lancaster Ave., Suite 102
Downingtown, PA 19335
cbmt.org

HORTICULTURAL THERAPIST

Contributed by Nancy Easterling, M.S.W., H.T.M.
President, American Horticultural Therapist Association
and Director, Horticultural Therapy Program
North Carolina Botanical Garden
University of North Carolina at Chapel Hill
and
Gaye Horton
Executive Director, American Horticultural Therapist Association

The Work of Horticultural Therapists

Horticultural therapy is a new and emerging field in rehabilitation services. It includes a broad range of programs that focus on vocational, social, or therapeutic outcomes for clients. Horticultural therapists engage clients in horticultural activities to achieve their treatment goals. The horticultural process itself is considered the therapeutic activity rather than the end product.

Horticultural therapists are specially educated and trained professionals who involve clients in any phase of gardening—from growing plants to selling them—as a means of improving their life. As members of treatment teams horticultural therapists develop goals and work plans to help each client improve skills and maximize abilities.

The benefits of horticultural therapy can be seen in the cognitive, psychological, social, and physical areas of clients' lives. For example, the cognitive benefits of horticultural therapy include the following:

Improving concentration and memory
Improving ability to achieve goals
Improving problem solving
Learning new terms/concepts
Following simple to complex instructions
Improving ability to plan
Taking steps, in proper order, to achieve an outcome
Improving judgment

The psychological benefits of horticultural therapy include the following:

Improving quality of life
Increasing self-esteem
Reducing stress
Improving mood
Increasing sense of control
Increasing sense of pride and accomplishment
Improving ability to deal with frustration
Increasing feelings of belonging or a sense of place

The social benefits of horticultural therapy include the following:

Improving ability to get along with others
Improving ability to work in groups
Improving cooperation and sharing
Increasing sense of responsibility
Developing nurturing skills
Developing healthy leisure pursuits
Improving skills in conflict resolution

The physical benefits of horticultural therapy include the following:

Decreasing heart rate
Improving fine and gross motor skills and eye-hand coordination
Increasing strength
Increasing endurance
Increasing range of motion
Reducing muscle tension
Decreasing perception of pain
Improving balance

People of all ages and special needs can benefit from involvement in horticultural therapy. As a result, horticultural therapy programs are found in a variety of health-care, rehabilitative, and residential settings such as:

Vocational, prevocational, occupational, and rehabilitation programs
Psychiatric hospitals and mental health programs
Substance abuse programs
Hospitals, clinics, and skilled nursing facilities
Hospice programs
Cancer centers
Correctional facilities
Shelters for the homeless and victims of abuse
Public and private schools
Assisted living and senior centers
Adult day-care centers
Community and botanic gardens

Although horticultural therapy is a relatively new therapeutic field, there are more than one thousand programs in operation today. AHTA provides links on its website to numerous resources about horticultural therapy and horticultural therapy programs, including community and botanic garden programs (ahta.org/links). These are excellent resources to learn more about what horticultural therapists do and about their careers.

Where Horticultural Therapists Work

The number of horticultural therapy and therapeutic horticulture programs has clearly increased over the past decade. You might have seen "healing gardens" featured in magazines. The American Horticultural Therapy Association (AHTA) developed the first therapeutic garden characteristics in 1995 and awarded the first Therapeutic Garden Design Award in 1997.

AHTA has worked with the American Society of Landscape Architects (ASLA) to develop healing gardens across the country. More and more of these gardens are being built in health-care settings.

How to Qualify to Become a Horticultural Therapist

There are universities, colleges, and community colleges that offer classes, certificates, and degrees in horticultural therapy. You can pursue a bachelor's degree, an associate degree, a certificate, or individual course work in horticultural therapy. However, to become professionally registered as a horticultural therapist, you must meet the following educational requirement:

A bachelor's degree in horticultural therapy or a bachelor's degree in another field and twelve semester hours of the following course work if not part of your chosen degree program:

Developmental Psychology
Abnormal Psychology
Human Growth and Development
Adult Development and Aging
Aspects of Disabilities and Illnesses
Group Dynamics
Principles of Therapy

Human Anatomy/Physiology
Medical and Psychiatric Terminology
Professional Ethics
Assistive Technology

Twelve semester hours of horticulture course work from the following areas:

Introduction to Horticulture
Plant Materials
General Plant Pathology
Pest and Disease Management
Plant Propagation
Floral Design
Greenhouse or Nursery Production/Management
Landscape Design

Nine semester hours of horticultural therapy course work from the following areas:

- Overview of the profession, which includes the definition of horticultural therapy, the history of horticultural therapy, and program types
- Horticultural therapy populations, which include physical disabilities, developmental disabilities, and mental/psychological disabilities
- Horticultural therapy programming and techniques, which include goals and objectives for horticultural therapy programs; client assessment, evaluation, and documentation tools; horticultural therapy programming activities; adapting programming activities to meet diverse client needs; and adaptive tools and devices
- Program management, which includes preparing proposals for horticultural therapy programs, developing a program budget, grant-writing overview, and research overview
- A minimum of four hundred-eighty hours of fieldwork supervised by a registered horticultural therapist

AHTA offers voluntary professional registration as an HTR—Horticultural Therapist Registered.

What Can You Earn as a Horticultural Therapist?

Like other therapy fields covered in this chapter, the average salary for horticultural therapists is estimated to be $36,600. The salary range is $30,700 to $43,200.

How to Advance as a Horticultural Therapist

Future opportunities are expected to be good for people trained as horticultural therapists because they work as members of medically oriented teams. The traditional career path of promotion to supervisor or director is sometimes open to you in this field. Advanced degrees and certification will qualify you to teach and do research at colleges and universities. As is true of many art, music, and dance therapists, some horticultural therapists write scholarly and technical publications to advance the field and enhance their professional reputation.

Additional Sources of Information

American Horticultural Therapy Association
201 E. Main St., Suite 1405
Lexington, KY 40507-2004
http://ahta.org

Canadian Horticultural Therapy Association
70 Westmount Rd.
Guelph, ON N1H 5H8
Canada
chta.ca

RECREATION THERAPIST

Recreation therapists are other possible members of treatment teams. Their special role on such teams is to foster, educate, and encourage patients to participate in leisure activities. These activities are designed to facilitate the patient's recovery or adjustment to an illness, injury, disability, or emotional condition.

The Work of Recreation Therapists

Therapeutic recreation specialists have the responsibility for planning, organizing, and directing recreation programs that have been medically approved. The programs can include adapted sports, games, arts, crafts, music, field trips, and social activities. The content of each program is determined in consultation with other members of the treatment team after the recreation therapist assesses a patient's talents, interests, and current abilities.

The primary purpose of the recreation therapist's work is either to restore a prior level of skill or to develop new leisure skills and activities. This is important to the overall recovery process because the recreation therapist is able to help patients attain not only a skill but also a quality of life that is personally satisfying.

Like other members of the treatment team, recreation therapists must prepare detailed reports. These reports describe each patient's reactions to the planned activities. They also include physical and emotional symptoms that manifest themselves before, during, or after participation in an activity. Other therapies and/or the recreational activities need to be adapted or changed in response to the patient's reactions.

Recreation therapists work with patients recovering from physical and mental illness. They can be children, teenagers, or adults. In addition, recreation therapists work with the elderly and provide them with opportunities for exercise, mental stimulation, creativity, and fun.

Special populations such as the terminally ill, the blind, the hearing impaired, children with learning disabilities, substance abusers, prison inmates, and juvenile offenders might also be served by recreation therapists. As in other therapeutic career fields, recreation therapists tend to specialize in treating certain groups and/or disabilities. Because much of their work is carried out as group activities, specialization is very important.

Where Recreation Therapists Work

The majority of recreation therapists work in comprehensive hospitals or in psychiatric hospitals. An increasing number are working in nursing homes and residential facilities. Recreation therapists are also employed in community mental health centers, adult day-care programs, local parks and recreation departments, special education programs, drug treatment centers, and correctional institutions.

A few recreation therapists are self-employed. They work under contract with organizations such as nursing homes or community agencies. They either provide recreation therapy for the organization's clients or develop and oversee programs for the agencies.

How to Qualify to Become a Recreation Therapist

The basic requirement for entering the field of recreation therapy is a bachelor's degree in therapeutic recreation or in recreation with a concentration in therapeutic recreation. These programs of study require course work in human anatomy, physiology, abnormal psychology, medical and psychiatric terminology, characteristics of illnesses and disabilities, the concepts of mainstreaming and normalization, professional ethics, and assessment and referral procedures. In addition, recreation therapists take courses in therapeutic recreation theory and practice, program design and management, professional issues, and a three hundred-sixty-hour clinical internship under the direct supervision of a certified recreation therapist.

The National Council for Therapeutic Recreation Certification is the organization that certifies recreation therapists and therapeutic recreation assistants. Certified recreation therapists must hold at least a bachelor's degree in recreation therapy and pass the certification examination. Therapeutic recreation assistants must hold at least an associate degree.

The council also accredits undergraduate and graduate programs of study in colleges and universities. There are more than sixty accredited programs in the United States.

What Can You Earn as a Recreation Therapist?

In 2007, the Health Careers Center (http://mshealthcareers.com/index.htm) reported the average annual salary of recreation therapist to be $34,100. The salary range was $22,600 to $41,300, where higher levels of education and experience are related to higher salaries.

How to Advance as a Recreation Therapist

Most recreation therapists work as members of a medically oriented team; therefore, the demand for recreation therapists is expected to grow steadily, particularly in the areas of outpatient care, assisted living, and rehabilitation facilities. Like other therapeutic fields, experienced recreation therapists can become supervisors and directors of recreation therapy in hospitals, clinics, and agency programs. If they are employed in small hospitals or clinics, they can move to larger organizations.

A few recreation therapists move from salaried positions in hospitals to private practice. As in the case of physical and occupational therapists, this trend is expected to increase as many agencies begin to use contract services to provide specialized health-care delivery. Recreation therapists with advanced degrees also teach and do research in higher education.

Additional Sources of Information

American Therapeutic Recreation Association
1414 Prince St., Suite 204
Alexandria, VA 22314
atra-tr.org

Canadian Therapeutic Recreation Association
P.O. Box 203, 5170 St. Patrick St.
Montreal, PQ H4E 4N5
Canada
canadian-tr.org

National Council for Therapeutic Recreation Certification
7 Elmwood Dr.
New City, NY 10956
nctrc.org

National Therapeutic Recreation Society
22377 Belmont Ridge Rd.
Ashburn, VA 20148
nrpa.org/branches/ntrs.htm

SPEECH-LANGUAGE PATHOLOGIST AND AUDIOLOGIST

Contributed by Marie E. Jetté, SLP-CCC
Center for Laryngeal Surgery and Voice Rehabilitation
Massachusetts General Hospital

Some people are born with hearing, speech, and/or language disorders. Others suffer loss of hearing, speech, or language as a result of illness, injury, or severe emotional stress. Speech-language pathologists and audiologists are the professionals who work with them.

The Work of Speech-Language Pathologists and Audiologists

Speech-language pathologists diagnose and treat people who have difficulties with communication. These difficulties can include hearing loss, an inability to make speech sounds or understand language, poor and irregular rhythm and fluency (stuttering), and improper pitch. Some speech-language pathologists also work with individuals who have difficulty eating and swallowing. Other speech-language pathologists are responsible for helping people with underdeveloped social skills.

Using special instrumentation and other testing devices, professionals in this area evaluate speech and language skills. In addition, they design, direct, and implement treatment plans to restore or improve a student or patient's communication ability. This can include counseling people with speech and language disabilities or serving as a consultant to educational or medical professionals who are important to the patient's rehabilitation.

Audiologists diagnose and treat people with hearing disorders. They evaluate the range, nature, and degree of hearing loss using special instrumentation such as audiometers. Like speech-language pathologists, audiologists design, direct, and implement treatment plans to help compensate for the patient's hearing loss. Audiologists fit patients for hearing aids and other mechanical devices to improve their hearing ability. Audiologists counsel their patients about their disability and the treatment they are receiving. They also serve as consultants to educational, medical, and other professional groups central to the patient's rehabilitation.

Some professionals in this area are trained in both speech-language pathology and audiology because there is a strong relationship between hearing and speech-language disorders. This combination of training allows these professionals to provide a complete treatment program for the patient.

Others in the fields of speech-language pathology and audiology teach the scientific principles of human hearing and communication. Others direct projects and conduct research in the areas of speech and hearing loss. These activities can be directed at developing new instrumentation to aid in the diagnosis of disorders. They can also be directed at the development of new equipment and instrumentation to help diagnose or restore all or part of a patient's hearing or speech loss.

Speech-language pathologists and audiologists usually specialize. There are many who work only with children, whereas others specialize in the diagnosis and treatment of adults.

Some speech-language pathologists specialize in the treatment of certain communication disorders such as stuttering, or voice or speech and language loss due to injury or illness. Likewise, audiologists also specialize in terms of the type of hearing disorder.

Speech-language pathologists and audiologists work in consultation with other professionals and the families of their patients. Speech-language pathologists and audiologists who work with children must maintain strong relationships with teachers and parents who will continue to help the child progress between treatment sessions. Similarly, speech-language pathologists who work with patients in a medical setting must communicate effectively with physicians, physical therapists, occupational therapists, and other medical professionals in order to adequately coordinate treatment.

Where Speech-Language Pathologists and Audiologists Work

Many speech-language pathologists and audiologists work in the public or private school setting. From preschool through high school, these professionals work with educators, doctors, and parents to facilitate learning for children with hearing and speech-language disorders.

A smaller percentage of speech-language pathologists and audiologists work in hospitals, rehabilitation centers, nursing homes, research labs, and for home health-care agencies. Some work in community clinics. Still others have private practices either alone or with other professionals.

How to Become a Speech-Language Pathologist or Audiologist

A master's degree is required to practice speech-language pathology, whereas practicing audiology now requires a clinical doctorate. The master's degree and supervised clinical experience, a passing score on a national examination, and a nine-month clinical fellowship following graduation are required for state licensure in most states. This training also qualifies the professional for certification by the American Speech-Language-Hearing Association. The certification is called the Certificate of Clinical Competency (CCC). Most professionals become certified in either speech-language pathology or in audiology. A very small percentage seek certification in both areas.

What Can You Earn as a Speech-Language Pathologist?

The 2007 report from the Health Careers Center reports that speech-language pathologists earn an average of $51,500. The salary range was $42,100 to $58,300. In 2007, the median salary for audiologists with one year of experience was $45,445 and for those with five to nine years of experience was $50,495.

How to Advance as a Speech-Language Pathologist or Audiologist

The job outlook for speech-language pathologists and audiologists is very good. Growth in employment opportunities is expected to grow faster than average because of advances in the field that can help the aging population as well as early identification for children.

As speech-language pathologists and audiologists gain experience, they often move from salaried positions in school systems and hospitals to private practice. This trend is expected to increase as public agencies downsize their staff and use contract services to provide health-care delivery.

Other speech-language pathologists and audiologists become directors and administrators of programs in schools, hospitals, and health-care or government agencies. Those with advanced degrees teach and do research in colleges and universities.

Additional Sources of Information

American Speech-Language-Hearing Association
10801 Rockville Pike
Rockville, MD 20852
asha.org

Canadian Association of Speech-Language Pathologists and Audiologists
920 - 1 Nicholas St.
Ottawa, ON K1N 7B7
Canada
caslpa.ca

CHAPTER 9

EDUCATIONAL SERVICES

As federal, state, and local governments put increased emphasis on education, the roles of the professionals represented in this chapter become increasingly important. Every child deserves the best education possible; however, some face challenges that need to be overcome in order to learn and grow. That makes the school psychologist, school social workers, school counselors, and college student affairs professionals important members of the academic team in schools, colleges, and universities. These professionals not only work with the students but with the parents, teachers, administrators, and community agencies to facilitate the academic and personal development of children and young adults.

The people in educational services occupations share much in common. They all

- Work in educational settings
- Are concerned about the education and overall well-being of children and young adults
- Deal with personal, psychological, social, academic, and/or career problems

While the settings, students, and techniques can differ, all are committed to helping students succeed. Responsibilities can include direct client services, program administration, and/or special instruction. Settings can include public and private elementary, middle, and high schools; special education facilities; rehabilitation and vocational centers; other special schools; and colleges and universities.

Some professionals work exclusively with preschool children. Others work with children with learning disabilities, children who are exhibiting antisocial behavior, or children who have been the victims of crime. Still others work with college students.

The occupations in this chapter represent an opportunity for people who are interested in both rehabilitation services careers and the education of students to combine their interests and abilities. Some of these occupations allow individuals to enter with a bachelor's degree. However, advancement in almost all of these occupations requires advanced degrees and numerous years of experience.

SCHOOL PSYCHOLOGIST

While the field of psychology offers a variety of career options, one of the more important is the school psychologist. School psychologists are members of the educational team who have an in-depth understanding of human intelligence and who have the expertise to measure mental capacity. Therefore, their role in the educational system generally focuses on diagnostic and remedial work with a range of students with special needs.

The Work of School Psychologists

School psychologists use the principles of clinical and educational psychology to work with students at all ages. These professionals become involved in diagnosing children with learning disabilities as well as gifted and talented students. They work with parents, teachers, and children to facilitate the educational success of children with special needs.

School psychologists are also involved in assessing and intervening on behalf of children with physical handicaps. They provide counseling to these students and consultation to their teachers and families. The Americans with Disabilities Act requires schools to adapt learning environments and provide services that allow students to learn and participate in mainstream classrooms.

In addition, school psychologists handle the social and emotional condition of children. They can use individual or group counseling sessions to help students cope with learning, behavioral, and emotional problems. They can also work in consultation with classroom teachers and parents to continue the progress being made in the counseling sessions.

Where School Psychologists Work

School psychologists are employed in public and private schools at the elementary, middle school, and high school levels. Some are employed in two-year and four-year colleges and universities, but the majority work with students in kindergarten through twelfth grade.

School psychologists who hold doctoral or master's degrees and have the necessary licensing for their geographic location can have private practices or work in clinics or state institutions. They can also work in human services and mental health clinics.

How to Become a School Psychologist

A master's degree in school or counseling psychology is a minimum qualification for the position of school psychologist. Some school psychologists even hold doctoral degrees. While it is not a necessary qualification, in almost every field of psychology, a doctorate is highly recommended. In some cases, it can also be important that the school psychologist graduate from a program approved by the American Psychological Association (APA). Some positions in large urban school systems can require graduation from an APA-accredited institution.

It's not always easy to find school psychology programs because at some universities, the school psychology program is in the school or college of education, and at other schools, the program is in the psychology department. A good tool for locating school psychology programs is the APA Guide to Graduate Study in Psychology (apa.org/gradstudy). Another good resource is the National Association of School Psychologists' Approved Graduate Programs in School Psychology (nasponline.org/certification/naspapproved.aspx).

What Can You Earn as a School Psychologist?

The 2007 salary survey conducted by PayScale.com reported that the median salary for school psychologists with one year or less of work experience was

$44,000. This means that half of the school psychologists participating in the salary survey made more than $44,000 and half made less. For school psychologists with five to nine years of experience, the median salary was $56,000.

How to Advance in Your Career as a School Psychologist

The demand for school psychologists is expected to grow faster than average through 2014, and shortages are expected due to this increased demand and expected retirements. Because many school psychologists are the only mental health professionals in their school setting, advancement to supervisor or director might not be possible. Some school psychologists can move from small schools to larger ones, and ultimately some can move to supervisory positions within the school district, state, or province. Those with doctoral degrees can teach and do research at colleges and universities. Those who become licensed psychologists can enter private practice and specialize in the educational and developmental problems of schoolchildren.

Additional Sources of Information

American Psychological Association
750 First St. NE, Suite 100
Washington, DC 20002
apa.org

Association of State and Provincial Psychology Boards
P.O. Box 241245
Montgomery, AL 36124-1245
asppb.org

Canadian Association of School Psychologists
10660 Trepassey Dr.
Richmond, BC V7E 4K7
Canada
cpa.ca/casp/index.html

National Association of School Psychologists
4340 East West Hwy., Suite 402
Bethesda, MD 20814
naspweb.org

SCHOOL SOCIAL WORKER

Within the field of social work, school social workers play an important role in the education of future generations. They apply their unique knowledge and skills of home, school, and community collaboration to the educational system. Their goal is to enhance the ability of teachers to teach and students to learn.

The Work of School Social Workers

Like psychology, the field of social work offers a variety of career options. School social workers deal with the problems of children in elementary, middle, or high school. They assist parents, teachers, and students in developing permanent solutions and/or coping strategies for these children to make them more able to learn.

School social workers play an important role in gathering data about the students with whom they work and the circumstances in which they live. They prepare family histories and interview all parties who play a significant role in the life of their students. School social workers can become involved in such issues as child abuse and neglect, teenage pregnancy, date rape, family conflicts, antisocial behavior, substance abuse, physical and mental disabilities, learning problems, illness, and poverty.

Using direct counseling and referral techniques, school social workers identify and consider solutions. They also find resources and information to improve the overall quality of life for children so that they can get the most from their educational experiences. Like other types of social workers, school social workers have to value the dignity and worth of each student and build a basis for trust and understanding.

Where School Social Workers Work

Like school psychologists, most school social workers are employed in public and private schools at the elementary, middle school, and high school levels. School social workers holding doctoral or master's degrees and having the necessary licensing for their geographic location can have private practices to work with children and their families in addressing education-related issues. Others with doctoral degrees teach and perform research at the university level.

How to Qualify to Become a School Social Worker

While a bachelor's degree in social work can be a sufficient requirement for a small rural school system, most social workers who are employed in public school systems must have a master's degree in social work. The graduate program of study that school social workers follow includes courses in human growth and development, social welfare policies, and methods of social work.

The master's degree for social workers interested in working in a school setting requires at least one year of experience in such a setting under the direct supervision of an experienced M.S.W. After two years of supervised experience as paid social workers, these professionals are eligible for membership in the Academy of Certified Social Workers.

What Can You Earn as a School Social Worker?

School social workers in their first year of work earned a median annual salary of $30,000 in 2007, according to PayScale.com. For those with five to nine years of experience, the median annual salary was $38,000.

How to Advance as a School Social Worker

Like school psychologists, a school social worker is usually the only social worker on the school staff. Therefore, advancement to supervisory positions within the school is rare. Those with the proper education and experience can be promoted to supervisor of school social workers for a district or for the state. It is also possible to move from a small school to a larger one and assume more responsibility.

Additional Sources of Information

Canadian Association of School Social Workers and Attendance
    Counsellors
76 Bluewater Crescent
Winnipeg, MB R2J 2P8
Canada
http://casswac.ca/default.asp

Council on Social Work Education
1725 Duke St., Suite 500
Alexandria, VA 22314
cswe.org
Publishes the *Directory of Accredited B.S.W. and M.S.W. Programs.*

National Association of Social Workers
750 First St. NE, Suite 700
Washington, DC 20002-4241
naswdc.org

School Social Worker Association of America
2 Pidgeon Hill Dr., Suite 340
Sterling, VA 20165
sswaa.org

SCHOOL COUNSELOR

School counselors are an important part of the educational community.
While they assist students in handling personal, family, and social problems, they also help students learn the skills needed to address problems
before they occur.

The Work of the School Counselor

School counselors assist students with their educational and career decisions. Their primary goal is to enhance the personal, social, and academic
growth of each student with whom they work.

To achieve this goal, school counselors emphasize preventive and developmental counseling by using a variety of strategies to work with their students. They interview students to assess personal needs, interests, and abilities. They conduct individual and group counseling sessions. They administer and interpret aptitude, interest, personality, and achievement tests. They also teach skills that help students manage their time better, conduct a more successful job search, prepare for interviews at colleges and universities as well as with employers, and reduce their level of test anxiety.

At the elementary school level, counselors often deal with social, behavioral, and personal problems on an individual basis. At the high school level, school counselors continue to handle these issues on either an individual basis or in groups. But at the high school level, counselors become increasingly more involved in assisting students as they make decisions about their future. These can include such important issues as employment on graduation, selection of an appropriate college and major, and/or marriage and family decisions.

School counselors consult with parents, teachers, school administrators, school psychologists, school nurses, and social workers. They also make referrals to medical, psychological, community, and law enforcement agencies.

Where School Counselors Work

School counselors work with students in kindergarten through twelfth grade. They are primarily employed in public and private schools. Some are employed in two-year and four-year colleges and universities.

School counselors who hold doctoral or master's degrees and have the necessary licensing can have private practices. They can also work in human resources and in mental health facilities. Those with doctoral degrees can teach and do research at the university level.

How to Qualify to Become a School Counselor

School counselors must have a master's degree in guidance and counseling or a master's degree in either elementary or secondary school counseling.

In some cases, school counselors are required to have a number of years of teaching experience prior to becoming a school counselor. In addition, more than half of all states require that school counselors be licensed, certified, or registered in order to work in the public school system.

The graduate course work that school counselors complete includes human growth and development, social and cultural foundations, helping relationships, individual and group counseling techniques, occupational information and career counseling, individual appraisal, and research and evaluation. School counselors also take courses in the history and philosophy of education. Graduate programs in counseling are usually accredited by the Council for Accreditation of Counseling and Related Educational Programs.

School counselors at large public and private schools that have several counselors on staff can become directors of guidance. They can also be promoted to directors or supervisors of guidance for their school, district, or state. Some school counselors can move from small schools to larger schools where their responsibilities may be expanded.

School counselors who pass state licensing requirements and become certified by the National Board for Certified Counselors can enter private practice. Often they will specialize in treating the problems of schoolchildren. Those who obtain a doctorate can become counselor educators who teach and conduct research at universities. Others consult with educators and business.

What Can You Earn as a School Counselor?

In 2007, the PayScale.com salary survey reported that the median salary for a school counselor with one year or less of work experience was $31,500. This means that half of the school counselors participating in the salary survey made more than $31,500 and half made less. For school counselors with five to nine years of experience, the median salary was $40,000.

How to Advance as a School Counselor

The majority of school counselors work as part of a guidance team in elementary, middle, and high schools. As part of this unique school staff, advancement is possible to assistant director and director positions where the school has a large guidance staff. It is possible to be promoted to the position of counseling or guidance supervisor for a school district after a number of years of experience.

Job opportunities for school counselors are expected to grow faster than average due to baby boom retirements and the increased birth rate in recent years. This means that opportunities for advancement will also increase.

Additional Sources of Information

American Counseling Association
5999 Stevenson Ave.
Alexandria, VA 22304
counseling.org

American School Counselor Association
1101 King St., Suite 625
Alexandria, VA 22314
schoolcounselor.org

Canadian Counselling Association
16 Concourse Gate, Suite 600
Ottawa, ON K2E 7S8
Canada
ccacc.ca

Council for Accreditation of Counseling and Related Educational
    Programs
1001 N. Fairfax St., Suite 510
Alexandria, VA 22314
cacrep.org

National Board for Certified Counselors
3 Terrace Way
Greensboro, NC 27403
nbcc.org

COLLEGE STUDENT AFFAIRS PROFESSIONAL

College student affairs professionals handle all phases of college life beyond the classroom. Some of the types of positions that might be classified under this occupational field include the following:

- **Dean of students.** This person administers college or university policy that pertains primarily to student services and student behavior. The dean of students also plans, implements, and evaluates programs designed to provide services to the student body. In general, other student affairs professionals report to the dean of students. In some cases, the dean of students can also have the title of vice president for student affairs. In large colleges and universities, these tend to be two different positions.
- **Career counselor.** This person assists students and alumni in obtaining jobs in their career field. Placement counselors work with business and industry as well as with the students and faculty. They set up campus interviews and prepare students for the job search process.
- **Counselors.** These professionals provide services to students who are experiencing adjustment problems, emotional problems, and/or academic difficulties.
- **Resident hall coordinators.** These people oversee campus life in the dormitories. Their responsibilities can include assigning rooms, training volunteer residence hall advisers, planning educational and social programs, and dealing with emergencies that occur.
- **Student center personnel.** These people manage campus student centers, which often contain dining facilities, bookstores, recreational facilities, meeting rooms, and student organization offices. Some positions in student centers are strictly administrative. These are issues of policy, budget, and personnel. Other positions are programmatic. They address the planning and implementation of special student programs and events.
- **Student advisers.** These people advise special groups of students on personal, social, and academic matters. They supplement the work of the student's academic adviser, who is generally a faculty member responsible for advising the student on appropriate courses to take. These special student advisers work with certain groups of students such as foreign students, minority students, female students, adult students, disabled students, and sorority and fraternity members.

• **Financial aid counselors.** These people assist students in obtaining federal, state, local, and institutional funding to pursue their education.

• **Admissions officers.** These people review the applications to attend the college or university and make decisions regarding who will be admitted each year.

• **Registrar.** This person maintains the academic records of all students. Each record includes all of the grades that a student has received throughout his or her college career. It can also include any disciplinary actions taken against the student.

Where College Student Affairs Professionals Work

Student affairs professionals work in colleges and universities. Some specialize in working with students attending community colleges, junior colleges, and two-year colleges. Others work for public and private four-year colleges and universities.

How to Qualify to Become a College Student Affairs Professional

The minimum requirement for a position in college student affairs is a bachelor's degree. If you have a bachelor's degree, you could qualify to be an admissions or financial aid counselor. However, a bachelor's degree will greatly limit your career options on any college campus. Most college student affairs professionals hold at least a master's degree in higher education administration, counseling, educational psychology, or a related area. Student affairs professionals with doctoral degrees tend to hold upper-level administrative positions or counseling positions.

There are no licensing or certification requirements for college student affairs professionals. However, members of college counseling centers must be graduates of doctoral programs in psychology that are approved by the American Psychological Association. In addition, these counselors can be licensed psychologists where they practice.

What Can You Earn as a College Student Affairs Professional?

Student affairs professionals with advanced degrees and entering their first year of work on a college or university campus had a median annual salary of $28,500 in the 2007 PayScale.com survey. For those with five to nine years of experience and advanced degrees, the median annual salary was $36,000.

Individuals at the director level in college student affairs had a median annual salary of $46,000. For those who become vice president of college student affairs, the median annual salary increased to $86,000.

How to Advance as a College Student Affairs Professional

In many areas of college student affairs work there is real opportunity for career progression because opportunities are increasing at a faster than average rate due to retirements and growing college enrollments. Coordinator or assistant positions generally require only a bachelor's degree on entry. However, with increased levels of experience and education, which is often available at the institution with a tuition waiver, it is possible to advance to counseling and administrative positions.

People with doctorates and numerous years of experience are qualified for the highest levels of college administration. They can also teach and do research as part of the college or university faculty. Some student affairs professionals go to federal or state government positions in departments of education.

Additional Sources of Information

ACPA—College Student Educators International
One Dupont Cir., Suite 300
Washington, DC 20036
acpa.nche.edu

American College Counseling Association
5999 Stevenson Ave.
Alexandria, VA 22304
collegecounseling.org

American College Personnel Association
One Dupont Cir. NW, Suite 300
Washington, DC 20036-1188
acpa.nche.edu

American Counseling Association
5999 Stevenson Ave.
Alexandria, VA 22304
counseling.org

Canadian Association of College and University Student Services
4 Cataraqui St., Suite 310
Kingston, ON K7K 1Z7
Canada
cacuss.ca/en/index.lasso

National Association of Colleges and Employers
62 Highland Ave.
Bethlehem, PA 18017-9085
naceweb.org

CHAPTER

10

SPECIAL SERVICES

Careers in social and rehabilitation services can be pursued in a range of settings and can address a variety of challenges that people face. In the previous chapters, we have demonstrated the diversity of responsibilities, settings, people served, training required, and patterns of advancement. This chapter offers a brief overview of some of the unique occupations in the field of social and rehabilitation services.

CHRISTIAN CLERGY AND JEWISH RABBINATE

It is human nature to believe that there is a power bigger than us. From the beginning of humanity, there have been people who have served our spiritual needs. In our society these people are primarily ministers, priests, and rabbis. They hold a special place in our communities because of the counsel and comfort they provide.

The Work of Clergy and Rabbis

Religious leaders of all faiths conduct regular worship services and administer religious rites, such as weddings and funerals, in accordance with the teachings of their faith. They also counsel members of their congregations who are in need of spiritual advice. In addition, they teach and interpret the doctrine of their religion through sermons and religious education classes.

They bring comfort to the sick; likewise, bereaved members of the congregation look to the clergy or the rabbi for counsel during their times of loss and anguish.

Some religious leaders publish their interpretations of the faith in books and articles. Others participate in interfaith organizations as well as civic, educational, and recreational activities.

Where Clergy and Rabbis Work

Most clergy and rabbis work in synagogues, churches, or parishes. Some work as missionaries, taking the teachings of their faith to many parts of the world. Others work as chaplains in the military, in hospitals, and on college campuses. Some teach in universities and in seminaries.

How to Qualify to Become a Member of the Clergy or a Rabbi

Every religion has a unique program to prepare those who plan to enter a religious vocation. The content of each program varies, but all clergy and rabbis must have a thorough knowledge of the beliefs and practices of their faith.

Some preparation can take three to five years. At the conclusion, a bachelor's degree is awarded. In other cases, there are no formal requirements. Many people who plan to enter the religious profession begin by learning the basic teachings of their faith early in life. Others come to the realization that they have a calling to religious life as adults. Sometimes these individuals have education and careers in very different fields. It is then necessary for them to complete a formal program of religious education.

What Can You Earn as a Member of the Clergy or as a Rabbi?

Earnings of clergy are low in comparison to other professional social and rehabilitation career fields. For example, Catholic priests earn salaries between $13,000 and $16,000. While this is very low, it's important to remember that the parishes in which priests work provide housing, food, and transportation for their priest.

Protestant ministers and rabbis tend to earn more than priests. Recent reports place their salary range between $50,000 and $100,000.

How to Advance as a Member of the Clergy or as a Rabbi

People who pursue spiritual careers do not do so for the advancement possibilities. However, new ministers, priests, and rabbis usually begin by assisting another clergy member or rabbi. With experience, they assume more responsibility for their congregations.

Within each religion there is a hierarchy of religious leadership. In addition to embodying the values of the faith, those who reach higher levels of spiritual leadership within their faith usually have advanced training or education as well as experience.

Additional Sources of Information

Canadian Association for Pastoral Practice and Education
7960 St. Margaret's Bay Rd.
Ingramport, NS B3Z 3Z7
Canada
cappe.org

Hebrew Union College
Jewish Institute of Religion
One W. Fourth St.
New York, NY 10012
huc.edu

Jewish Theological Seminary of America
3080 Broadway
New York, NY 10027
jtsa.edu

National Coalition for Church Vocations
5420 S. Cornell Ave. #105
Chicago, IL 60615-5604
nccv-vocations.org

PROBATION OFFICER/PAROLE OFFICER

Probation and parole officers are a unique group of social workers who participate in the formulation and development of plans to release juvenile and adult offenders from correctional institutions. They provide supervision for offenders who have been released, and they develop a regular plan of treatment and follow-up during the time of probation or parole.

The Work of Probation and Parole Officers

Probation and parole officers secure necessary services for offenders including education and employment. They also make referrals to other social services agencies and rehabilitation services professionals who provide necessary services to offenders.

It is important that a probation or parole officer establish a good working relationship with the offender to gain a thorough understanding of his or her personal history before, during, and after incarceration. Working with the family of the offender can also be an important part of rehabilitation.

Probation and parole officers also make recommendations to the courts on sentencing and parole. They can return an offender to a correctional institution if the individual is not adhering to the conditions of his or her parole or probation.

The traditional casework methods of social work are very important in this occupation. Direct counseling, securing services, making referrals, and conducting follow-up are all important tasks performed by probation and parole officers.

Where Probation and Parole Officers Work

Probation and parole officers work for the court system. Generally, they are employed by correctional institutions or parole agencies.

How to Qualify to Become a Probation or Parole Officer

A bachelor's degree in social work, rehabilitation services, sociology, psychology, or another social science is good preparation for a career as a probation or parole officer.

What Can You Earn as a Probation or Parole Officer?

The 2007 salary survey conducted by PayScale.com reported that the median salary for probation officers with one year or less of work experience was $32,000. This means that half of the parole officers participating in the salary survey made more than $32,000 and half made less. For parole officers with five to nine years of experience, the median salary was $38,800.

How to Advance as a Probation or Parole Officer

Probation and parole is a career field that is expected to experience faster than average growth through 2014. This means that more officers will be able to advance to supervisory positions. Those with the proper education and experience can be promoted to direct an agency. It is also possible for probation and parole officers to move from a small agency to a larger one and assume more responsibility.

Additional Sources of Information

American Probation and Parole Association
2760 Research Park Dr.
P.O. Box 11910
Lexington, KY 40578
csom.org/about/p_appa.html

National Council on Crime and Delinquency
685 Market St., Suite 620
San Francisco, CA 94105
cascomm.com/users/nccd

REHABILITATION AIDES

The field of rehabilitation services offers numerous opportunities to work as an aide in a variety of occupations and settings. Aide positions are very accessible for those who want to be part of the rehabilitation services career field but do not have the experience and/or the educational requirements for professional positions.

Rehabilitation aide positions generally do not have a specific education requirement. Employers prefer at least some high school education, and a high school diploma is considered very helpful if the position is a full-time one.

Aides in social and rehabilitation services usually have completed lower levels of education and receive lower levels of pay. In 2007, PayScale.com reported that social and rehabilitation aides received between $9 and $16 per hour. This calculates to an annual salary of between $18,700 and $33,300.

There is a growing demand for rehabilitation services. As the population ages, as people with disabilities enter the mainstream of life, and as educators take on the responsibility of educating the whole child, there will be an increasing demand for people who can assist the professionals in the field. Therefore, the number of aide positions is expected to grow in the future. The following are only a few of the possibilities that exist for rehabilitation aides.

Geriatric Aide

In this highly rewarding but demanding job, geriatric aides assist and care for the elderly. Geriatric aides work with rehabilitation services professionals who specialize in caring for the elderly, whose conditions can range from critically ill to relatively healthy. The professionals with whom geriatric aides work include doctors, nurses, physical therapists, occupational therapists, speech specialists, nutritionists, recreation specialists, social workers, and rehabilitation counselors.

The responsibilities of a geriatric aide can include feeding, bathing, dressing, and accompanying the elderly. Some geriatric aides monitor the medical status of elderly patients. Others assist in recreational activities.

The duties of geriatric aides are as varied as the settings in which those duties are carried out. Aides work in medical, therapeutic, recreational, and transportation settings. They can be employed in hospitals, nursing homes, adult day-care centers, recreational programs, and private homes.

There are new and emerging college degree programs that focus on working with the elderly. There are also graduate programs that prepare people to direct gerontology programs. A person can begin as a geriatric aide and with time, experience, and advanced education can assume increasing amounts of responsibility in this growing field.

To advance from the position of geriatric aide, it is necessary to pursue additional education in a related area. Nursing school can prepare a person to be a geriatric nurse. A bachelor's degree in an area such as social work, rehabilitation services, psychology, or sociology can open a variety of options, including medical school. Specialized training can also lead to a position as a medical assistant.

Additional Sources of Information
American Geriatrics Society
Empire State Bldg.
350 Fifth Ave., Suite 801
New York, NY 10118
americangeriatrics.org

Psychiatric Aide
Psychiatric aides have demanding positions, but these can be highly rewarding jobs. Through their day-to-day activities in helping patients with their personal care or assisting them in getting to and from their treatments and activities, psychiatric aides are often the ones to see a patient experience small personal triumphs.

Under the close supervision of the professional staff, psychiatric aides measure vital statistics, collect laboratory specimens, draw blood, administer medications, and perform other routine nursing procedures. They help patients and their families adjust to hospitalization. They motivate and encourage the patient to follow the treatment plan and to participate in activities that the medical team has prescribed.

They are important to the professional team because they observe and record important information on the reactions and symptoms of the patients. It is often the psychiatric aide who first observes important changes in behavior. Therefore, psychiatric aides need to be very good at record keeping.

Psychiatric aides primarily work in psychiatric hospitals and the psychiatric units of large hospitals. Some work in community mental health programs, residential facilities, nursing homes, and drug treatment centers.

While a high school diploma is not required, often the psychiatric aide receives training on the job. These training programs can last a few days or a few months. Some community colleges offer courses that prepare psychiatric aides. The course work includes anatomy, physiology, medical terminology, nutrition, and communication skills.

To advance from the position of psychiatric aide, it is necessary to pursue additional education. Some psychiatric aides go on to nursing school, while others go on to college and obtain an undergraduate degree in an area such as psychology, social work, or rehabilitation services. Some continue their education in graduate programs such as counseling, psychology, or social work; others go on to medical school.

Physical and Occupational Therapy Aides

Working with physical and occupational therapists, these aides prepare patients for their treatments. They also assist during the administration of the treatments by adjusting equipment, encouraging the patient, and securing the patient in specialized equipment. In some cases, physical and occupational therapy aides may provide routine treatment, but they always work under the close supervision of a licensed certified therapist.

Like other aides, physical and occupational therapy aides work very closely with patients. They assist them in dressing and in removing or putting on prosthetic or orthotic devices. As the patients practice their exercises, the aides observe and record data on the results of the treatment.

Physical and occupational therapy aides maintain an inventory of equipment and supplies. They are also responsible for keeping the equipment clean and in working order.

Aides in this field work side by side with the physical or occupational therapist. Therefore, they work in hospitals and rehabilitation centers. However, more aides will be needed in home health agencies, nursing homes, hospices, sports medicine centers, athletic departments of colleges and universities, and fitness programs in business and industry as the demand for therapists in these settings increases. Physical and occupational therapists in private practice can employ aides to work with them as well.

During high school, the best preparation for becoming a physical or occupational therapy aide is course work in biology and psychology. This is also good preparation for continuing one's education beyond high school as a means to advance to the position of a physical or occupational therapist.

C H A P T E R

11

CAREER PATHS AND UPWARD MOBILITY

This book demonstrates the wide range of career paths that are available to people in social and rehabilitation services. What your career path will look like depends on the occupation you select and on your personal interests, abilities, needs, and values. However, there are five basic traits that successful individuals exhibit:

1. They set long-range goals but stay open to unexpected opportunities.
2. They accept that failures will happen; they learn from them and move on.
3. They avoid self-intimidation and don't set grandiose goals and overwhelming challenges.
4. They do not set limited work hours. Your employer pays for and must get forty hours a week of your time and commitment. Every other hour that you work is an investment in yourself and your career development.
5. They tend to verbally attribute achievements to "luck" but inwardly hold a strong belief in their own power to overcome challenges.

These traits are as true for social and rehabilitation services careers as any other career field. While some occupations within the field of rehabilitation services might not offer what is commonly thought of as career progression, the traits of successful people will probably result in career success however the occupation or individual defines it.

For example, new professionals who enter a particular field, such as art therapy, might not anticipate being promoted from a staff position to a supervisory and then to an executive position. They will define their success in terms of their clients' successes, their own professional reputation, or an expanding practice. However, in other areas of rehabilitation services, promotion might be a realistic expectation.

Movement between agencies is a common path to higher-level responsibility. In addition, many occupations within rehabilitation services offer the ability to enter private practice. This is another career path that many people in rehabilitation services follow. It is important to look at the types of career paths that are available in your profession and in your geographic location. However, the basic keys to career mobility and advancement in the field of social and rehabilitation services are education, experience, and certification and licensure.

CLINICAL CAREERS

The chapters on mental health services, medical services, and therapeutic services each describe clinical occupations in the rehabilitation services field. These occupations all demand education beyond the bachelor's degree. In some cases, a master's degree is the minimum level of education required for entry. In other cases, a doctorate or professional degree, such as a medical degree, is required.

However, education alone is not sufficient for people entering clinical careers. They must also have years of supervised clinical experience under the direction of other certified and licensed professionals. In some fields this is paid experience, and in other fields it is unpaid. It is important to gather all of the information available on the nature and duration of the clinical experience that is required in your area of interest.

Clinical careers all demand that you pass a certification examination and, in many cases, a separate licensing examination. These examinations are administered by both professional organizations in the field and licensing boards in the states where you plan to practice.

Because the public places such a high degree of trust in social and rehabilitation services professionals who pursue clinical careers, there is a demanding process for entry and advancement. This is a necessary protection for both the public and the professional. Once certified and licensed, it is imperative that you continue to take courses on a regular basis to stay current in your field and to renew the certification and licensing.

ADMINISTRATIVE CAREERS

The first key to pursuing an administrative career in rehabilitation services is obtaining the proper education, certifications, and licensure. Generally this requires a master's degree in an area such as the following:

- Rehabilitation counseling
- General counseling
- Mental health counseling
- Social work
- Counseling psychology
- Sociology

Although these graduate programs prepare you for the clinical work of your profession, they do not actually prepare you for the administrative responsibilities of a supervisor or agency director. However, career advancement in the area of administration can be very rapid after completion of a master's degree, particularly a rehabilitation counseling degree. Studies have shown that within as few as eighteen months of completing a master's in rehabilitation counseling, a significant percentage of people are promoted to supervisory or administrative positions. The vast majority of these graduates reach managerial positions within less than five years of graduation.

In supervisory positions the responsibilities may still be very closely related to the delivery of client services. In addition, a supervisor of rehabilitation counseling or social work counselors will be responsible for a staff of counselors and social workers who provide individual and group counseling services to the clients.

Supervisory responsibilities are quite different from those of the agency director, even though both may hold the same degree in counseling or social work. The director or agency administrator is responsible for such areas as fiscal management, program planning and evaluation, public relations, and marketing services. An agency director also has ultimate responsibility for managing counseling and noncounseling personnel. The size of the agency plays a significant part in determining the amount of contact the director or administrator has with clients.

Success as a supervisor or agency director will depend on your ability to master many leadership and management competencies. These can include the following:

Vision and purpose
Managerial courage
Aligning and motivating others
Building effective teams
Hiring and developing staff
Interpersonal communication skills
Intellectual rigor
Professional presence
Integrity and trust
Leveraging resources
Change and adaptability
Business acumen

Different agencies will place different value on these leadership competencies, but all agencies will require many of them. If you are in a position where you need to develop some of these competencies in order to advance, it would be good to find appropriate continuing education courses in business or public administration. Some social and rehabilitation professionals return to school for an M.B.A. or a master's in public administration in order to bring higher-level leadership skills to their agency.

How Decisions Are Made

Decisions about career advancement in administrative positions in rehabilitation services fields are often made by the agency's board of directors. Studies have shown that these boards tend to evaluate candidates for administrative positions on six major criteria:

1. Prior experience and success in management and supervision
2. An academic degree appropriate to the agency's mission and goals (This is usually a master's degree, but sometimes a doctorate is preferred.)
3. A history of career advancement with evidence of leadership skills and initiative
4. A stable employment history
5. Evidence of interest in the mission and goals of the agency through paid or volunteer experience
6. A well-conducted interview for the position and excellent references

EDUCATION: YOUR KEY TO ADVANCEMENT

The field of rehabilitation services offers a wide range of opportunities, from aides to physicians. However, graduate or professional education is the real key to career mobility, if not advancement, in this field. To determine if you should be planning to pursue a graduate or professional degree, ask yourself the following questions:

Do I have a real interest in the subject I am planning to study?

Am I trying to advance my skills in this particular area?

Do I have a real desire to help others?

Does my career field require graduate education?

If you can answer yes to one or more of these questions, the next step is to select a college or university with the type of graduate or professional program that suits your needs. There are numerous directories of colleges and universities that will give you a listing of the institutions and the types of programs that they offer.

Identifying Graduate and Professional Programs

A good directory will provide information on such things as the faculty/student ratio (it should be low), the number of master's and doctoral degrees awarded annually, the percentage of women and minorities admitted, whom to contact for application materials, and what standardized tests are required.

Standardized Tests and Graduate or Professional School

While medical schools require the Medical College Admissions Test (MCAT), graduate programs in most other areas of rehabilitation services require the Graduate Record Examination (GRE) or the Miller's Analogies Test (MAT). It is advisable to take these tests during your senior year of college, even if you are not planning to go on to graduate school. The scores are good for five years, and many people have changed their plans and decided to go to graduate school after being out of college a few years. It is difficult to review all of the material, particularly the mathematics portion of the exam, when you have not been in school for several years.

Completing the Application

Graduate applications usually require basic information about you and your undergraduate record. The application package includes the following:

- An application form
- An official transcript of your undergraduate courses and grades
- Usually three letters of reference, preferably from faculty members who can comment on your academic ability
- A statement of purpose—why you want to pursue graduate study and what you have to offer to the program
- Your request for financial assistance

Unlike undergraduate admissions, which are reviewed and evaluated in the admissions office, graduate applications are reviewed and evaluated by the faculty members who will teach you and work with you. Therefore, before you apply it is advisable to learn all you can about the faculty in the department. Where are their degrees from? What is their area of expertise? What books and articles have they published? Are they interested in the same things that interest you? These are important questions.

Paying for Graduate or Professional School

There can be more options available for graduate students than undergraduate students when it comes to paying for graduate programs. While student loans are available to graduate students, there are often other sources of financial assistance that are unique to graduate study, including the following:

- **Teaching assistantships.** These provide stipends, and sometimes tuition waivers, to full-time graduate students for assisting a faculty member in teaching undergraduate classes.
- **Research assistantships.** These provide stipends, and sometimes tuition waivers, to full-time graduate students for assistance on a faculty research project.
- **Fellowships.** These provide money to full-time graduate students to cover the costs of study and living expenses and are not based on an obligation to assist in teaching or conducting research.

In most graduate programs, these forms of financial assistance are very competitive. It is important to have a good undergraduate record and evidence of a commitment to the field. The commitment can be evidenced in the form of paid related work experience or volunteer experience. The faculty committee that reviews applications for this type of financial assistance needs to see that you can make a substantive contribution to their work.

ORGANIZATIONAL CULTURES AND THEIR IMPORTANCE TO YOUR CAREER DEVELOPMENT

On completion of your education or training program you will enter an organization or agency that will have its own unique culture. The staff members will have a way in which they communicate, both formally and informally. This form of communication may be different among peers than it is with supervisors and administrators. As the new person on staff, you might have very little power to change this culture; therefore, it is important to assess the environment before accepting the position. If you don't, you greatly increase the probability of failure on the job should your values and the culture of the organization clash.

There will be indications of the culture in the description of the job and in the way interviewers describe their organization or agency during the interview. Do they emphasize a team approach or independent work? Do they demonstrate a basic respect for their clients/patients? Are their mission and goals compatible with their programs or treatments? What is the turnover rate of their professional staff? Do they promote from within?

These are some of the issues you will want to assess. You will also want to meet with as many professional staff members as possible during your initial interview or any subsequent interviews to determine if there is a good fit between you and the organization. When you are asked if you have any questions, be prepared! It is then your turn to evaluate the employer. Ask such questions as the following:

What are the opportunities for personal growth?
Tell me how your team works together to serve patients/clients.
Could you describe a typical career path in this agency?
How will I be evaluated?
How frequently has the position for which I am being considered
    turned over in the last five years?
Tell me about the agency's plans for the next three years.
What are the financial challenges that the agency is facing?
What makes your agency different from others that do the
    same thing?
Describe the management style of your organization.
Describe the work environment.
Why do you enjoy working here?
What characteristics does a person need to be successful here?

Keep in mind that the most important aspect of personal and professional growth is a positive mental attitude about yourself: your strengths, your weaknesses, your skills, your abilities, and your interests. This is the fundamental building block of any successful career. When you have a clear picture of your own potential, it is easier to plan and pursue a career that is compatible with your interests and abilities as well as your needs and values.

CHAPTER 12

INTERNATIONAL HUMANITARIAN WORK

Contributed by Ann McLaughlin, M.S.W.
Director, NGOabroad

Often when we hear about globalization or international work, we think about manufacturing and jobs being outsourced to other countries. However, many people in social and rehabilitation services careers would like to apply their skills and knowledge to the problems that face people around the world. If you are one of those people, this chapter will help you understand what the international issues are, how you need to prepare yourself, and which organizations can help you achieve your goal.

THE FOCUS IS POVERTY

Many people think that international work is all about the conflict zones. Wrong! That's just where the TV camera crews film. Though there is humanitarian work in Darfur and Afghanistan, the most important work to be done revolves around poverty. Twenty-five percent or one-quarter of all humanity lives in poverty.

According to the World Summit for Social Development and Beyond:

- 1.2 billion people—a quarter of the human race—are living in conditions of almost unimaginable suffering and want.

- Between 600 and 700 million children, representing about 40 percent of all those in the developing world, are currently struggling to survive on less than one dollar a day.
- Nearly one billion people in the world are illiterate.
- Approximately 1.3 billion people lack safe water. Over half of the developing world's population (2.6 billion people) is without access to adequate sanitation.
- If the world were to invest an extra thirty cents out of every one hundred dollars, all children would be healthy, well nourished, and in primary school.
- Studies in more than thirty countries indicate basic social services receive, on average, between 12 and 14 percent of total public spending. Two-thirds of these countries spend more on debt servicing than on basic social services; several spend three to five times more on debt.

Humanitarian work is devoted to responding to these unmet human needs.

SKILLS MOST NEEDED

What kinds of skills are most needed? Because of the large percentage of people living in poverty, humanitarian work focuses on improving quality of life:

- Nurses, nurse midwives, nurse practitioners
- Doctors (less demand for dentists and pharmacists)
- Social workers, counselors, youth workers
- Community organizers
- Public health—sanitation and water engineers
- Teachers and tutors, especially in the area of literacy
- Business development—finance, accounting, and micro-finance
- Agriculture, nutrition
- Human rights, law
- International relations, conflict resolution

- Vocational training
- Women's rights

What additional skills are needed in jobs or on a voluntary basis?

- Working with children and youth
- Physical and occupational therapists
- Disability experts and advocates
- Builders and people in the trades
- Immigrant and refugee advocates
- Domestic violence workers
- Theater, writing, music, and photography teachers
- Entrepreneurial or income-generating skills, such as hair stylists, auto or motorbike mechanics, bakers, restaurateurs, importers/exporters
- Sports (a way to connect with youth and build confidence)
- Fund-raising and project development
- Media and radio broadcasting
- Appropriate technology (e.g., solar electricity, stoves that do not use wood)
- Photography, the arts, theater
- Teaching journalism
- Teaching computer skills
- Teaching English

THE GREAT DIVIDE

The biggest step that most humanitarian workers will take is not onto the plane to their first assignment, but across the great divide—from a rich country to poor; from flushing toilets to raw sewage; from glistening hospitals to no medical care at all.

Employers look for adaptable, resourceful workers who can "hit the ground running" and who don't whine about boiling their water, long bus rides, or boring Saturday nights "in the middle of nowhere." Employers look for people who can gracefully make the leap across the great divide.

Thus, people who have firsthand knowledge of the everyday life struggles in Asia, Africa, or Central and South America are at a distinct advantage. They know the beliefs, the perspectives, the history, the customs, and the language of the people.

What if you do not have these cultural roots? Immerse yourself. One young man hung out at the house of his best friend from India as much as he could so that he would feel very at home in Indian culture.

International humanitarian work is competitive because people from all over the world apply for a single position. To get a job, you must persevere. When most people think of humanitarian work, they are thinking of the enormous need for help, not the enormous number of people competing for a limited number of jobs.

NONGOVERNMENTAL ORGANIZATIONS (NGOs)

International NGOs are relief organizations. CARE was one of the first big international relief organizations. CARE would send "CARE packages" and also bring in food for famine relief. CARE, like most NGOs, has expanded its services and its reach over the years.

Recently, 136 nongovernmental organizations (NGOs) responded to the deadly 2004 Indian Ocean tsunami, which killed more than seventeen thousand people. Some of these NGOs included Ireland's Trocaire, HelpAge to assist the elderly, Taiwan Buddhist Tzu Chi Foundation, and Mercy Corps.

The good news is that all over the world, grassroots organizations are sprouting. Today, there are many kinds of programs in NGOs that help in the following areas:

• **Women.** The World Bank and United Nations organizations now recognize that if you want to uplift a nation, it is critical to improve the lives of women. What is the logic? All over the world, women care for the children and so are most invested in improving health and education.

In Africa, girls have been excluded from education. No longer. Nelson Mandela asked Oprah Winfrey to fund a girl's school in South Africa. This is just the beginning. I predict that we will see more NGOs devoted to the education of girls.

- **Literacy and income generation.** These are important poverty alleviation programs.
- **Refugees.** Thankfully the number of conflicts in the world is decreasing, so there are fewer refugees and internally displaced people, but there is still a huge need for services.
- **Health.** Services offered include public health and medical services, nursing, and physical and occupational therapies.
- **Sanitation and appropriate technology.** In most of the poor world, only a quarter of the people have electricity. Solar power is now being used to power the essential buildings in a village. Pipes are being laid so that people have access to clean water and various kinds of stoves reduce the need to forage for firewood and also prevent respiratory problems.
- **The environment.** Environmental NGOs interface with appropriate technology. For example, the United Nation's Environment Program funded a project in Nairobi's largest slum, Kibera, to develop an oven that burns trash—not trees—for cooking use. Thus, the slum is being cleaned up, and trees are making a comeback.
- **Social services.** Drama, art, sports, and music are more often the venues to help with socio-emotional wounds, such as with child soldiers. Talk therapy as we know it in the West is often not culturally appropriate. Social services are often lacking in poor countries, and services for elders or the disabled are rare or nonexistent.

Over the next five or ten years, job opportunities in NGOs will increase because international humanitarian work is burgeoning. NGOs are becoming important new players internationally. It was the NGOs, not governments, that were center stage after the 2004 tsunami, after Pakistan's earthquake of 2005, and after Hurricane Katrina in the United States.

POVERTY DETERMINES THE PRIORITIES

Many of the people seeking opportunities in international humanitarian work innocently assume that life in Nairobi is similar to life in the United States, and so is the job scene. Think again. Most impoverished nations have a small fraction of the resources of the United States; therefore, they have a lot less social services infrastructure.

There may be the need for all social and rehabilitation services, but the country may not be able to afford to provide all of those services. For example, there is only one physician for every ten thousand people in most African countries, and other professionals are equally rare. Though your services are desperately needed, you can never take a job from a native of the country in which you work. Therefore, your niche as a foreign or expatriate worker must be with one of the international humanitarian organizations. International work is determined by both need and the availability of the infrastructure.

Teachers, vocational trainers, social workers, community organizers, and religious professionals help establish infrastructure and address the roots of poverty. Speech and language therapists and physical and occupational therapists are desperately needed but relatively rare because, as mentioned before, most impoverished nations cannot afford the doctors that would lead the treatment teams.

Art, drama, dance, and recreation therapists are held in high regard internationally. Why? These action-oriented therapies transcend language and culture. In contrast, mental health counseling is based on a European Freudian model. Talk therapy is just too European for most cultures.

Substance and addictions counselors are needed in many countries. However, few poor countries have any services for alcohol or drug abuse.

You see? There are overwhelming needs but few rehabilitation or social services—yet. In our lifetimes, let us see what we can do to address those human needs.

GETTING YOUR FOOT IN THE DOOR

How do you get your proverbial foot in the international service door?

• Grasp the societal needs of the countries you are interested in. Know the history and culture of many countries to help figure where you are needed. If you were a social worker, art therapist, nurse, or doctor working with AIDS, where would you most likely work in Central America? Which war-torn countries might need help with prosthetics? The ability to answer such questions helps you knock on the right doors.

- Corollary: which countries need your skills? If you are a physical therapist, where are you needed? How would you figure this out? Clue: What are the needs or problems that a physical therapist addresses? Where would you find people with those needs?

- Don't limit your options. If you know that you want to work in mental health in Honduras, it's important to know that social services are organized differently in other countries. Most countries cannot afford mental health services. Honduras might have more pressing social needs. (You guessed it: those pressing needs revolve around poverty.)

- Craft what you offer around urgent human needs. Answer the urgent needs or problems in a country, in a company, or in an organization. This is the secret to getting a job at home or in another country.

- Start on the bottom rung. Many people are disappointed that they do not get a response to their application from Save the Children, UK. Big organizations must get thousands of applications per day! It is probably best to start with smaller NGOs that work in Africa, or the country of your choice.

- Practical skills and interests can be as important as your education and professional skills. Gritty, grubby practical skills are as valuable as the skills acquired in school. For example, skills in laying pipe are valued everywhere women must walk miles with jars on their head to get water from a well or bore hole. Agricultural skills from the Plains or the Prairies gain you points in Mongolia and the Pampas. Know how to repair lobster boats in Maine or Nova Scotia? Such marine construction skills were needed after the tsunami. If you have taught swimming, done fund-raisers, worked with kids with disabilities, or are athletic, musical, or theatrical, note these talents on your resume. They distinguish you; they help you connect across cultures and are valuable skills.

- Employers look for attitude. They hire team players who roll up their sleeves and ask, "How can I help?" and ignore self-serving sycophants who ask, "How can I get a job?"

- Are your emotional loose ends tied up? Or will a recent romantic breakup or the death of a loved one hit you when you step off the plane? Don't let the lure of international work outweigh safety or reality considerations.

- Do not seek placements that are over your head. Organizations invest time and energy to get you up to speed. Approach international work in a graduated way: start with objectives that are easy for you, then increase the challenge as you gain confidence and skills.

• "Test drive your skills before you leave the parking lot." Learn your professional skills at home and contribute them abroad. Do not expect to learn the rudiments of your craft abroad; you will have your hands full adjusting to a new culture.

• Be well versed in current events and regional history so you do not step into danger. Consular Affairs (voyage.gc.ca), the U.S. State Department's Travel Advisory (http://travel.state.gov/), and Human Rights Watch (hrw .org) are all excellent sources about safety, as are natives of your desired countries.

• Do your homework. Many people blow past these critical preparation steps: learning the historical and cultural background, the customs and beliefs so they can gracefully ease in to a country and better understand the glitches that they encounter; and knowing to bring a malaria tent—how to stay safe and healthy. Do you know how to prevent gastrointestinal problems? How to drink clean water when there is none to be found? How to not get worms, bed bugs, or dengue fever? Doing your homework is smart.

• Don't strike out on your own. Cavalier students equipped with only brief information from a website and plane tickets are asking for trouble. Consult with college career advisers or international advising services or participate in established programs.

POSSIBLE FUTURES

International work is changing very quickly. Who and what will likely impact international humanitarian work? What might be different by the time you graduate and have your degree?

• **Bill Gates.** If Bill quits Microsoft and devotes himself to philanthropy, he might change international humanitarian work, especially medical care in Africa, as much as he has developed software and transformed information technology.

• **China.** China has made strong trade ties with South America and Africa and ensured that oil can flow across Central Asia. China is now generating its own NGOs and allowing international NGOs into China. If the international job search is now tight for humanitarian workers, what will it be like when China, a nation of one billion, enters the race?

• **NGOs.** NGOs, especially in Africa, are bypassing governments. African governments were not providing health care or education. NGOs are stepping in to fill the gap. Formed by the people, NGOs are more responsive to human needs.

• **"Make Poverty History."** As intercultural connections increase, people in the Northern Hemisphere are becoming aware that our brothers and sisters in the Southern Hemisphere are living in abject poverty. Conversely, through TV and the Internet, people in the South are becoming acutely aware that people in the North live in relative luxury. Both sides of the great divide are now pushing to eliminate poverty. The awareness raised by new communication systems could change how power and privilege are stacked.

In your lifetime, the nature of humanitarian work will dramatically change. If poverty can be eliminated, then what will be the focus of humanitarian work? Your generation will determine that answer. "Your mission, if you should decide to undertake it" is huge.

A FINAL THOUGHT

By incrementally building the necessary professional, cultural, international, and language skills, you can position yourself to enter into international work. Whether as a social worker working with AIDS orphans, an occupational therapist working with developmentally delayed children in Romania, or a vocational trainer helping create jobs in the slums where one-quarter of humanity lives, international humanitarian work is one of the most exciting emerging careers!

C H A P T E R

13

THE IMPACT OF LEGISLATION AND TECHNOLOGY

Technology and legislation are two major areas that constantly impact social and rehabilitation services. Few other fields are as susceptible to changes in these areas.

Consider that many of the employment opportunities in this career field are tied closely to government funding. Changes in legislation can open and close opportunities in the field very quickly. Look on any professional association's website and you will find pages and links devoted to legislative issues of importance to that particular field. In addition, you will notice that most have located their headquarters in the Washington, D.C., area. In Canada, many associations have strong presence in each province. They know how important legislative priorities and government funding can be to the careers of their members and to their patients and clients. They want to be close at hand to represent the interests of their members and the members' patients/clients.

Likewise technology and advances in science impact the treatment and care for patients/clients. With the technological explosion of the last thirty years, many social and rehabilitation services occupations have had to change their professional standards of care to keep pace. As researchers identify new techniques and new technologies for the rehabilitation of many disabling conditions, continuing education is becoming increasingly important.

LEGISLATIVE HISTORY AND ITS IMPACT ON REHABILITATION SERVICES

Over the past century a series of laws has been passed in Washington, D.C. Each piece of legislation defined the term *disability* and described how the federal government expected the states to serve those who were determined to be disabled. Each piece of legislation also funded specific activities in the area of rehabilitation services.

The initial legislation was aimed at the rehabilitation of war veterans. The scope of the original legislation was limited to rehabilitating veterans for entry into the workforce. The federal government gave funds to each state to take care of its own veterans through the state's vocational education board.

Today, organizations such as Disabled American Veterans (DAV) continue to monitor legislation concerned with veterans' benefits. Their staff of social and rehabilitation professionals also provide counseling and claims representation to veterans and their families, emergency relief for disabled veterans, and scholarships for children of needy disabled veterans. These staff members also advocate for local employment programs and removal of architectural and other barriers in the home and workplace.

Subsequent laws expanded not only the definition of disabled but also the populations that could be served. Later laws included nonveterans with severe physical and mental disabilities as well as mental retardation. The laws also broadened the scope of services beyond job placement. There was legislation that funded medical services, including surgery; counseling services for the disabled and their families; construction of facilities for persons with various types of disabilities; and education and training of a wide variety of rehabilitation services professionals.

Passage of the Americans with Disabilities Act (ADA) has continued the process of bringing disabled citizens into the mainstream of American life. By targeting employment, transportation, public service, and communications, this act has broadened the scope of services available to people with disabilities. It has also expanded the responsibilities of both rehabilitation services professionals and the business community in addressing the needs of the physically and mentally disabled.

The ADA has led to the development of organizations like Job Accommodation Network (JAN). JAN was originally sponsored by the President's Committee on Employment of People with Disabilities. It provides businesses with information and consultation on government policies and recommended worksite modifications (jan.wvu.edu). Rehabilitation experts are working not only with clients with disabilities but also with the organizations that employ them. The goal is to ensure that the workplace accommodates people with disabilities so that they can make a productive contribution to their employers and to society.

The National Rehabilitation Association was just one of many social and rehabilitation services associations that played an active role in the passage of the ADA. Since its passage, these professionals have observed new opportunities for employment, socialization, and community participation created by the ADA for people with disabilities. However, they feel that more needs to be done because of the continued high unemployment rate among people with disabilities. Therefore, they remain active in the legislative process.

On the international scene, Rehabilitation International (rehab-international.org) is a federation of more than one hundred organizations in eighty-nine countries. Rehabilitation International lobbies for legislation on issues of disability prevention and rehabilitation worldwide, thus creating various opportunities for social and rehabilitation services professionals around the world.

Welfare to Work (WtW) legislation, passed during the Clinton administration in the 1990s, was designed to help welfare recipients and other low-income Americans move into full employment. WtW helps the hardest-to-employ recipients of welfare assistance to prepare for employment, find jobs, and stay employed. It has greatly increased the opportunities for social and rehabilitation services professionals to work in the areas of employment readiness and placement.

THE IMPACT OF TECHNOLOGY ON REHABILITATION SERVICES PROFESSIONALS AND THE PEOPLE THEY SERVE

The impact of technology on the rehabilitation services field is unlimited. Every day, advances in technology make the work of social and rehabilitation services professionals easier and improve the quality of life for their clients.

Today, agency administrators are able to computerize client records, transmit reports to other members of the treatment team via electronic mail systems, and prepare agency payrolls. Employment services professionals are able to use computerized job searches and career-interest inventories with clients who previously were unable to access such assistance.

In the area of physical therapy, computer-based technology is being used to stimulate the muscles in the legs of paraplegic patients, allowing them to walk and ride bicycles. Electronic sensors and computer-based systems are now available to allow a quadriplegic person to communicate through a computer. As a result of further adaptation, these systems now allow patients to control the functions of a robotic arm by blinking their eyes.

Laser surgical techniques also hold new promise for many people with disabilities. Such surgeries as hip replacements have become almost commonplace due to advances in technology and robotic surgical equipment. This means that many elderly workers can increase the duration of their time in the workforce.

With the introduction of computer-aided design, work and living areas can now be planned and adapted for persons with disabilities. In fact, there is now an interdisciplinary group of rehabilitation engineers, occupational and physical therapists, and others in the rehabilitation field who are concerned with providing modern technology to persons with disabilities. The group is known as the Rehabilitation Engineering and Assistive Technology Society of North America (RESNA). The RESNA mission statement is clear. "Our purpose is to improve the potential of people with disabilities to achieve their goals through the use of technology. We serve that purpose by promoting research, development, education, advocacy and provision of technology; and by supporting the people engaged in these activities." (resna.org).

It is increasingly important that new professionals in the field of social and rehabilitation services are knowledgeable about the capabilities and limitations of technology as it applies to social and rehabilitation services areas. Their expertise in psychology, human development, anatomy, and recovery will be vital to the full implementation of technology to the benefit of their clients.

The Trace Research and Development Center at the University of Wisconsin (http://trace.wisc.edu) was formed in 1971 to address the communication needs of people who are nonspeaking and have severe disabilities. The Center was an early leader in augmentative communication.

Later, the Trace Center became a leader in making personal computers accessible to people with all types of disabilities and developed computer design guidelines that have become the basis for many industry guidelines and accessibility standards. Trace Center continues to work with companies to integrate disability access features into most operating systems and computer environments today, making them more accessible to and usable by the elderly and people with disabilities.

HOW TO READ THE TEA LEAVES

While technology and legislation may appear to be far removed from rehabilitation services, those who are considering a career in this area should be aware of just how these two phenomena can impact their career. It is important to keep up with current events through radio and television, the Web, magazines, and newspapers.

Increased attention is being paid to the health-care delivery system in this country. How will the actions in Washington, D.C., and your state capital impact the career field in which you are interested? Will recommended legislation limit or expand your earning potential? Will it provide more or fewer opportunities for you to pursue your education in your chosen field? How will it impact employment opportunities in that field?

It is also important to be knowledgeable about advances in technology that impact the occupations and the clients in which you are interested. It is important to become more aware of the emerging technologies in your field through education and training opportunities outside of school and/ or elective courses in school. Having this knowledge can make you more competitive in a competitive job market.

You might be thinking that you don't like computers and technology. After all, you are a people person. However, consider whether you will be able to be truly helpful to the people you decide to serve if you do not stay current about the capabilities of the new technologies.

Social and rehabilitation services careers offer challenge, responsibility, and reward to those who are well prepared and willing to work hard on behalf of the people they want to help.

CHAPTER

14

PROFESSIONAL LICENSURE AND CERTIFICATION

All rehabilitation services professionals have a legal obligation to perform their professional duties in a manner that is the same as all other professionals in the field. Any professional who fails to do this when providing services to clients/patients can be legally charged with malpractice or negligence.

In these instances, the court or the jury will determine whether or not the professional standard of care was breached. In most cases the "standard of care" is set by the appropriate professional organization and/or the state's licensing board for the particular occupation.

Laws and regulations concerning all forms of rehabilitation services have drastically increased in recent years. For this reason, clients/patients are expecting more and better services from rehabilitation services professionals. People entering any occupation in this field should not only be well prepared in terms of theory and technique but also in terms of the federal and state laws that pertain to the standards of care for that particular occupation.

In addition, it is advisable to become familiar with the ethical standards and guidelines that are prepared by the professional organizations in the appropriate field. These are easily available by writing to the appropriate organization.

In almost all areas of rehabilitation services, licensure and certification assure the public, and other professionals, that those holding such credentials are knowledgeable of and subscribe to the professional standards of care for their particular occupation. In some occupations it is not possible to be employed without these credentials.

WHAT IS LICENSURE?

Most states have established licensure boards to preserve the health, safety, and welfare of the public. They represent a state's best effort to establish appropriate standards for a wide variety of professionals. To become a private practitioner in many of the rehabilitation services fields it is necessary to be licensed by, and abide by, the regulations of the appropriate state licensing board for that occupation.

In general, licensure requires that certain educational requirements have been met and that a certain number of hours of supervised clinical experience have been completed as part of the educational program of study. In many occupational fields, licensure also requires that a candidate have a specified number of years of experience working under the direct supervision of another licensed professional. Finally, licensure requires the passage of a written exam, and sometimes an oral exam.

While the doctorate is the highest level of educational attainment for a rehabilitation services professional, the licensed professional in any of these fields will have attained one of the highest levels of standing in that profession. Licensing of rehabilitation services professionals is a way for the public to know who has met the extensive and specific professional standards of the licensing board.

Licensing boards may revoke a person's license if there is just cause to do so. Just cause may include conviction of a felony or misdemeanor involving moral turpitude, gaining a license by fraud or misrepresentation, conducting a practice where the ability to practice safely is in question, negligence in professional conduct, or not conforming to the standards of practice for that profession.

WHAT IS CERTIFICATION?

Certification promotes professional responsibility, accountability, and visibility. It enables the public to identify those counselors who have met the professional standards set forth by the appropriate credentialing bodies.

Certification is intended to protect the public from those who are not qualified to provide a particular form of rehabilitation service. It also provides a referral network for the public.

Through the registry of certified rehabilitation services professionals, the public has access to counselors, therapists, and practitioners who have the professional accountability and recognition awarded to them by the appropriate certifying agency. The certification means that each professional in the registry has successfully fulfilled the educational and/or experiential requirements for certification.

The purpose of certification organizations is to provide the public with the assurance that professionals engaged in their particular practice of rehabilitation services have met the established standards of preparation at the time that they enter the profession. Periodic renewal of certification assures that these standards are maintained throughout the professional's career.

Certifying organizations establish and monitor certification systems appropriate to their particular fields. In addition, they identify and register those professionals who have voluntarily sought and gained certification.

Certification is generally awarded for a specific period of time. Completion of a specified number of hours of continuing professional education is required to renew the certification at the conclusion of this time. This assures that professionals are keeping up-to-date with changes in their field. The intent of any certification process is to provide a national standard of performance and professional behavior in the field.

WHO NEEDS CERTIFICATION AND LICENSURE?

Anyone who offers medical, therapeutic, and/or counseling services to the public needs either a license or certification, or both. In some occupations you must be licensed and certified before you can be employed in an agency or organization. In other occupations, licensure and certification are required only if you intend to enter private practice.

It is important to learn all you can about the requirements of your field of interest. It is also important that you stay informed because licensure and certification requirements can change over time. You always want to know what your occupational field demands.

WHO PROVIDES IT?

Depending on the occupational field, certification is usually provided by the appropriate professional organization or a subsidiary of that organization. Many professional associations have established separate certification boards to handle this aspect of their members' professional life.

Licensure of rehabilitation services professionals is done through state licensure boards or committees. These agencies license a wide variety of professionals. Each group has its own examining and licensure board. These boards are made up of licensed professionals in the field; they monitor the examination and licensure process and hear cases to revoke the license of a professional in the field.

COUNSELOR STATE LICENSURE BOARDS

Alabama

Board of Examiners in Counseling
950 22nd St. N., Suite 765
Birmingham, AL 35203
abec.state.al.us
Licensed Professional Counselor (LPC)
Associate Licensed Counselor (ALC)

Alaska

Board of Professional Counselors
P.O. Box 110806
Juneau, AK 99811-0806
commerce.state.ak.us/occ/ppco.htm
Licensed Professional Counselor (LPC)

Arizona

Board of Behavioral Health Examiners
3443 N. Central Ave., Suite 1700
Phoenix, AZ 85012
bbhe.state.as.us
Licensed Professional Counselor (LPC)
Licensed Associate Counselor (LAC)

Arkansas

Board of Examiners in Counseling
P.O. Box 70
Magnolia, AR 71754
state.ar.us/abec
Licensed Professional Counselor (LPC)
Licensed Associate Counselor (LAC)

California

No licensure is required.

Colorado

Board of Licensed Professional Counselor Examiners
1560 Broadway, Suite 1350
Denver, CO 80202
dora.state.co.us/mental-health
Licensed Professional Counselor (LPC)
Provisional Licensed Professional Counselor

Connecticut

Office of Practitioner Licensing and Certification
410 Capitol Ave., MS #12APP
P.O. Box 340308
Hartford, CT 06134-0308
ct-clic.com
Licensed Professional Counselor (LPC)

Delaware

DE Board of Professional Counselors of Mental Health and
    Chemical Dependency Professionals
Cannon Building
861 Silverlake Blvd., Suite 203
Dover, DE 19904-2467
professionallicensing.state.de.us
Licensed Professional Counselor of Mental Health (LPCMH)
Licensed Associate Counselor of Mental Health (LACMH)

District of Columbia

Board of Professional Counseling
717 14th St. NW, Suite 600
Washington, DC 20005
http://hpla.doh.dc.gov/hpla/site/default.asp
Licensed Professional Counselor (LPC)

Florida

Board of Clinical Social Work, Marriage and Family Therapy,
    and Mental Health Counseling
4052 Bald Cypress Way, BIN C-08
Tallahassee, FL 32399
doh.state.fl.us/mqa
Licensed Mental Health Counselor (LMHC)
Provisional Mental Health Counselor
Registered Mental Health Counselor Intern

Georgia

Composite Board of Professional Counselors, Social Workers,
    and Marriage and Family Therapists
237 Coliseum Dr.
Macon, GA 31217
sos.state.ga.us.plb/counselors
Licensed Professional Counselor (LPC)
Associate Licensed Professional Counselor (ALPC)

Hawaii

Department of Commerce and Consumer Affairs—PVL
Mental Health Counselor Program
P.O. Box 3469
Honolulu, HI 96801
hawaii.gov/dcca/areas/pvl/programs/mental
Licensed Mental Health Counselor (LMHC)

Idaho

State Licensing Board of Professional Counselors and Marriage
and Family Therapists
1109 Main St., Suite 220
Boise, ID 83702
ibol.idaho.gov/cou.htm
Licensed Clinical Professional Counselor (LCPC)
Licensed Professional Counselor (LPC)
Registered Counselor Intern

Illinois

Professional Counselor Licensing and Disciplinary Board
320 W. Washington St., 3rd Floor
Springfield, IL 62786
idfpr.com/dpr/who/prfcns.asp
Licensed Clinical Professional Counselor (LCPC)
Licensed Professional Counselor (LPC)

Indiana

Social Worker, Marriage and Family Therapist, and Mental Health
Counselor Board
402 W. Washington St., Room W072
Indianapolis, IN 46204
in.gov/pla/bandc/mhcb
Licensed Mental Health Counselor (LMHC)

Iowa

Board of Behavioral Science Examiners
Lucas State Office Bldg., 5th Floor
321 E. 12th St.
Des Moines, IA 50319
idph.state.ia.us/licensure
Licensed Mental Health Counselor (LMHC)

Kansas

Behavioral Sciences Regulatory Board
712 S. Kansas Ave.
Topeka, KS 66603
ksbsrb.org
Licensed Clinical Professional Counselor (LCPC)
Licensed Professional Counselor (LPC)

Kentucky

Board of Licensed Professional Counselors
P.O. Box 1360
Frankfort, KY 40602
http://finance.ky.gov/bpc
Licensed Professional Clinical Counselor (LPCC)
Licensed Professional Counselor Associate (LPCA)

Louisiana

Licensed Professional Counselors Board of Examiners
8631 Summa Ave.
Baton Rouge, LA 70809
lpc.board.org
Licensed Professional Counselor (LPC)
Counselor Intern

Maine

Board of Counseling Professionals
35 State House Station
Augusta, ME 04333
maine.gov/pfr/olr
Licensed Clinical Professional Counselor (LCPC)
Licensed Professional Counselor (LPC)
Conditional LCPC
Conditional LPC

Maryland

Board of Examiners of Professional Counselors and Therapists
4201 Patterson Ave., 3rd Floor
Baltimore, MD 21215
dhmh/state/md.us/bopc
Licensed Clinical Professional Counselor (LCPC)
Certified Professional Counselor (CPC)
Licensed Graduate Professional Counselor

Massachusetts

Board of Allied Mental Health Professions
230 Causeway St., Suite 500
Boston, MA 02114
mass.gov/reg/boards/mh
Licensed Mental Health Counselor (LMHC)

Michigan

Board of Counseling
P.O. Box 30670
Lansing, MI 48909
michigan.gov/bhser
Licensed Professional Counselor (LPC)
Limited Licensed Professional Counselor (LLPC)

Minnesota

Board of Behavioral Health and Therapy

2829 University Ave. SE, Suite 210

Minneapolis, MN 55414

bbht.state.mn.us

Licensed Professional Counselor (LPC)

Mississippi

State Board of Examiners for Licensed Professional Counselors

P.O. Box 1497

129 E. Jefferson St., Suite 3

Yazoo City, MS 39194

lpc.state.ms.us

Licensed Professional Counselor (LPC)

Missouri

Committee for Professional Counselors

3605 Missouri Blvd.

P.O. Box 1335

Jefferson City, MO 65102

http://pr.mo.gov/counselors.asp

Licensed Professional Counselor (LPC)

Provisional Licensed Professional Counselor (PLPC)/Counselor In-Training (CIT)

Montana

Board of Social Work Examiners and Professional Counselors

301 S. Park, 4th Floor

P.O. Box 200513

Helena, MT 59620

swpc.mt.gov

Licensed Clinical Professional Counselor (LCPC)

Nebraska

Board of Mental Health Practice
P.O. Box 94986
Lincoln, NE 68509
hhs.state.ne.us/crl/mhcs/mental/mentalhealth.htm
*Licensed Mental Health Practitioner-Certified Professional
Counselor or Licensed Professional Counselor
(LMHP-CPC/LPC)*
Licensed Mental Health Practitioner (LMHP)
Provisional Licensed Mental Health Practitioner (PLMHP)

Nevada

No licensure is required.

New Hampshire

Board of Mental Health Practice
49 Donovan St.
Concord, NH 03301
state.nh.us/mhpb
Licensed Clinical Mental Health Counselor (LCMHC)

New Jersey

Board of Marriage and Family Therapy Examiners
Professional Counselor Examiners Committee
P.O. Box 45007
Newark, NJ 07101
state.nj.us/lps/ca/medical/familytherapy.htm
Licensed Professional Counselor (LPC)
Licensed Associate Counselor (LAC)

New Mexico

Counseling and Therapy Practice Board
2550 Cerrillos Rd.
Santa Fe, NM 87505
counselingboard@state.nm.us
Licensed Professional Clinical Mental Health Counselor (LPCC)
Licensed Mental Health Counselor (LMHC)

New York

State Board for Mental Health Practitioners
89 Washington Ave.
Albany, NY 12234-1000
op.nysed.gov/mhclic.htm
Licensed Mental Health Counselor (LMHC)

North Carolina

Board of Licensed Professional Counselors
P.O. Box 1369
Garner, NC 27529
ncblpc.org
Licensed Professional Counselor (LPC)

North Dakota

Board of Counselor Examiners
2112 10th Ave. SE
Mandan, ND 58554
edutech.nodak.edu/ndbce
Licensed Professional Clinical Counselor (LPCC)
Licensed Professional Counselor (LPC)
Licensed Associate Professional Counselor (LAPC)

Ohio

Counselor, Social Worker, and Marriage and Family Therapist Board
50 West Broad St., Suite 1075
Columbus, OH 43215
http://cswmft.ohio.gov
Licensed Professional Clinical Counselor (LPCC)
Licensed Professional Counselor (LPC)
Professional Counselor/Clinical Resident
Registered Counselor Trainee

Oklahoma

State Board of Licensed Professional Counselors
1000 NE 10th St.
Oklahoma City, OK 73117
health.ok.giv/program/lpc
Licensed Professional Counselor (LPC)

Oregon

Board of Licensed Professional Counselors and Therapists
3218 Pringle Rd. SE, Suite 250
Salem, OR 97302-6312
oblpct.state.or.us
Licensed Professional Counselor (LPC)
Registered Intern

Pennsylvania

State Board of Social Workers, Marriage and Family Therapists, and
    Professional Counselors
P.O. Box 2649
Harrisburg, PA 17105-2649
dos.state.pa.us/social
Licensed Professional Counselor (LPC)

Puerto Rico

Board of Examiners of Professional Counselors

P.O. Box 10200

San Juan, PR 00908

salud.gov.pr

Licensed Professional Counselor (LPC)

Professional Counselor with Provisional License (PCPL)

Rhode Island

Board of Mental Health Counselors and Marriage and
    Family Therapists

3 Capitol Hill

Providence, RI 02908

health.ri.gov/hsr

Clinical Counselor in Mental Health (CCMH)

South Carolina

Board of Examiners of Licensure of Professional Counselors, Marriage
    and Family Therapists, and Psycho-Educational Specialists

P.O. Box 11329

Columbia, SC 29211-1329

llr.state.sc.us/pol/counselors

Licensed Professional Counselor (LPC)

Professional Counselor Intern (PCI)

South Dakota

SD Department of Human Services

Board of Counselor Examiners

P.O. Box 1822

Sioux Falls, SD 57101

state.sd.us/dhs/boards/counselor

Tennessee

Board of Professional Counselors, Marital and Family Therapists,
  and Clinical Pastoral Therapists
227 French Landing, Suite 300
Nashville, TN 37243
http://health.state.tn.us
Licensed Professional Counselor–Mental Health Service Provider
  (LPC/MHSP)
Licensed Professional Counselor (LPC)

Texas

Board of Examiners of Professional Counselors
1100 W. 49th St.
Austin, TX 78756
dshs.state.tx.us/plc
Licensed Professional Counselor (LPC)
Licensed Professional Counselor Intern (LPC-I)

Utah

Professional Counselor Licensing Board
P.O. Box 146741
Salt Lake City, UT 84114-6741
http://dopl.utah.gov/licensing/professional_counselor/html
Licensed Professional Counselor (LPC)
Certified Professional Counselor Intern

Vermont

Board of Allied Mental Health Practitioners
Redstone Bldg.
26 Terrace St., Drawer 09
Montpelier, VT 05609-1106
http://vtprofessionals.org
Licensed Clinical Mental Health Counselor (LCMHC)

Virginia

Board of Counseling
6603 W. Broad St., 5th Floor
Richmond, VA 23230
dhp.virginia.gov/counseling
Licensed Professional Counselor (LPC)

Washington

Mental Health Counselor Program
P.O. Box 47865
Olympia, WA 98504-7865
doh.wa.gov/licensing/htm
Licensed Mental Health Counselor (LMHC)
Registered Counselor

West Virginia

Board of Examiners in Counseling
P.O. Box 129
Ona, WV 25545
wvbec.org
Licensed Professional Counselor (LPC)

Wisconsin

Examining Board of Marriage and Family Therapists, Social Workers,
   and Professional Counselors
P.O. Box 8935
Madison, WI 53708
http://drl.wi.gov/prof/coun/def.htm
Licensed Professional Counselor (LPC)
Professional Counselor Trainee

Wyoming
Mental Health Professions Licensing Board
1800 Carey Ave., 4th Floor
Cheyenne, WY 82002
http://plboards.state.wy.us/mentalhealth/index.asp

SOCIAL WORKER STATE LICENSURE BOARDS

Alabama
Board of Social Work Examiners
Folsom Administrative Bldg.
64 North Union St., Suite 129
Montgomery, AL 36130-1620
socialwork.alabama.gov

Alaska
Board of Social Work Examiners
Division of Occupational Licensing
P.O. Box 110806
Juneau, AK 99811-0806
dced.state.ak.us/occ/pcsw.htm

Arizona
Board of Behavioral Health Examiners
1400 W. Washington, Suite 350
Phoenix, AZ 85007
bbhe.state.az.us/lic%20sw.htm

Arkansas
Social Work Licensing Board
P.O. Box 250381
Little Rock, AR 72225
arkansas.gov/swlb.licensing_info.html

California

Board of Behavioral Sciences
400 R St., Suite 3150
Sacramento, CA 95814
bbs.ca.gov

Colorado

Social Work Examiners Board
1560 Broadway, Suite 1370
Denver, CO 80202
dora.state.co.us/mental-health

Connecticut

Department of Public Health
Clinical Social Worker Licensure
410 Capital Rd., MS #12APP
P.O. Box 340308
Hartford, CT 06314-0308
ct-clic.com/detail.asp?code=1775

Delaware

Board of Clinical Social Work Examiners
861 Silver Lake Blvd., Suite 203
Dover, DE 19904-2467
http://dpt.delaware.gov/boards/socialworkers/index.shtml

Florida

Department of Health
4052 Bald Cypress Way, BIN #C08
Tallahassee, FL 32399-3258
doh.state.fl.us/mqa/491/soc_home.html

Georgia

Composite Board of Professional Counselors, Social Workers,
    and Marriage and Family Therapists
237 Coliseum Dr.
Macon, GA 31217
http://sos.georgia.gov/plb/counselors

Hawaii

DCCA-PVL
Attn: SW
P.O. Box 3469
Honolulu, HI 96801
hawaii.gov/dcca/areas/pvl/programs/socialworker

Idaho

Board of Social Work Examiners
Bureau of Occupational Licensing
1109 Main St., Suite 220
Boise, ID 83702-5642
ibol.idaho.gov.swo.htm

Illinois

Social Work Examining and Disciplinary Board
Dept. of Professional Regulation
320 W. Washington St., 3rd Floor
Springfield, IL 62786
idfpr.com

Indiana

Indiana Social Worker, Marriage and Family Therapist and
    Mental Health Counselor Board
Health Professions Bureau
Indiana Government Center
402 W. Washington St., Room 041
Indianapolis, IN 46204
in.gov/pla/bandc/mhcb/licen_sw.html

Iowa

Board of Social Work Examiners
Bureau of Professional Licensure
Lucas State Office Building, 5th Floor
Des Moines, IA 50319-0075
idph.state.ia.us/licensure/board_home.asp?board=sw

Kansas

Behavioral Science Regulatory Board
712 S. Kansas Ave.
Topeka, KS 66603-3817
ksbsrb.org/social-workers.html

Kentucky

Kentucky Board of Social Work
P.O. Box 1360
Frankfort, KY 40602
http://finance.ky.gov/ourcabinet/caboff/oas/op/socwkbd

Louisiana

Louisiana State Board of Social Work Examiners
18550 Highland Rd., Suite B
Baton Rouge, LA 70809
labswe.org

Maine

State Board of Social Work Licensure
#35 State House Station
Augusta, ME 04333-0035
maine.gov/pfr/professionallicensing/index.shtml

Maryland

State Board of Social Work Examiners
Dept. of Health and Mental Hygiene
4201 Patterson Ave.
Baltimore, MD 21215
dhmh.state.md.us/bswe

Massachusetts

Board of Registration of Social Workers
239 Causeway St., Suite 500
Boston, MA 02114
mass.gov/

Michigan

Board of Examiners of Social Work
P.O. Box 30246
Lansing, MI 48909
cis.state.mi.us/bhser/lic/home.htm

Minnesota

Board of Social Work
2829 University Ave. SE, Suite 340
Saint Paul, MN 55414-3239
socialwork.state.mn.us

Mississippi

Mississippi State Board of Examiners for Social Workers and Marriage
and Family Therapists
P.O. Box 4508
Jackson, MS 39296-4508
msboeswmft.com

Missouri

State Committee for Social Workers
3605 Missouri Blvd.
P.O. Box 1335
Jefferson City, MO 65102-1335
http://pr.mo.gov

Montana

Board of Social Work Examiners and Professional Counselors
301 S. Park, 4th Floor
P.O. Box 200513
Helena, MT 59620-0513
http://mt.gov/dli/bsd/license/bsd_boards/swp_board/board_page.asp

Nebraska

Bureau of Examining Boards
301 Centennial Mall South
P.O. Box 95007
Lincoln, NE 68509
hhs.state.ne.us/crl/mhcs/mental/mentalhealth.htm

Nevada

Board of Examiners for Social Workers
4600 Kietzke Lane #C-121
Reno, NV 89502
http://socwork.nv.gov/forms.htm

New Hampshire

Board of Mental Health Practice
49 Donovan St.
Concord, NH 03301
nh.gov/mhpb

New Jersey

State Board of Social Work Examiners
P.O. Box 45033
Newark, NJ 07101
state.nj.us/lps/ca/social/swlic.htm

New Mexico

Board of Social Work Examiners
2055 Pacheco St., Suite 300
Santa Fe, NM 87504
http://rld.state.nm.us/b&c/socialwk/index.htm

New York

NY State Education Department
Office of the Professions
Division of Professional Licensing Services
Social Work Unit
89 Washington Ave.
Albany, NY 12234-1000
op.nysed.gov/csw.htm

North Carolina

Social Work Certification and Licensure Board
P.O. Box 1043
Asheboro, NC 27204
ncswboard.org

North Dakota

Board of Social Work Examiners
P.O. Box 914
Bismarck, ND 58502-0914
ndbswe.com

Ohio

Counselor and Social Work Board
77 S. High St., 16th Floor
Columbus, OH 43266-0340
http://cswmft.ohio.gov

Oklahoma

Board of Licensed Social Workers
3535 NW 58th
Oklahoma City, OK 73112
osblsw.state.ok.us

Oregon

Oregon State Board of Licensed Clinical Social Workers
3218 Pringle Rd. SE, Suite 240
Salem, OR 97302-6310
oregon.gov/BCSW/faq-lic.shtml

Pennsylvania

State Board of Social Workers, Marriage and Family Therapists
    and Professional Counselors
P.O. Box 2649
Harrisburg, PA 17105-2649
dos.state.pa.us/bpoa/cwp/view.asp?a=1104&q=433177

Puerto Rico

c/o NASW, Puerto Rico Chapter
271 Ramon Ramos Casellas St.
Urb. Roosevelt
Hata Rey, PR 00918

Rhode Island

Division of Health Services Regulation
Health Professions
3 Capitol Hill, Room 104
Providence, RI 02908
health.ri.gov/hsr/professions/s_work.php

South Carolina

Board of Social Work Examiners
P.O. Box 11329
Columbia, SC 29211
llr.state.sc.us/pol/socialworkers

South Dakota

Board of Social Work Examiners
135 E. Illinois, Suite 214
Spearfish, SD 57783
http://dhs.sd.gov

Tennessee

Board of Social Work
First Floor, Cordell Hull Bldg.
425 Fifth Ave.
North Nashville, TN 37247-1010
http://state.tn.us/sos/rules/1365/1365.htm

Texas

State Board of Social Work Examiners
1100 W. 49th St.
Austin, TX 78756-3183
dshs.state.tx.us/socialwork/default.shtm

Utah

Social Worker Licensing Board
160 E. 300 S.
P.O. Box 146741
Salt Lake City, UT 84114-6741
dopl.utah.gov/licensing/social_work.html

Vermont

Office of the Secretary of State
Licensing and Registration Division
109 State St.
Montpelier, VT 05609
http://vtprofessionals.org/opr1/social_workers

Virginia

Board of Social Work
6606 W. Broad St., 4th Floor
Richmond, VA 23230-1717
dhp.state.va.us/social/default.htm

Virgin Islands

Board of Social Work Licensure
No. 1 Subbase, 2nd Floor, Room 205
St. Thomas, VI 00802

Washington

Washington State Department of Health
Health Professions Quality Assurance
1300 SE Quince St.
P.O. Box 47860
Olympia, WA 98504-7860
https://fortress.wa.gov/doh/hpqa1/hps7/social_worker/
default.htm

Washington, D.C.

DC Department of Health
DC Board of Social Work
825 N. Capitol St. NE, Room 2224
Washington, DC 20002
http://doh.dc.gov/doh/site/default.asp

West Virginia

Board of Social Work Examiners
P.O. Box 5459
Charleston, WV 25361
wvsocialworkboard.org

Wisconsin

Board of Social Workers, Marriage Family
Therapists and Professional Counselors
Dept. of Regulation and Licensing
P.O. Box 8935
Madison, WI 53708-8935
http://drl.wi.gov/index.htm

Wyoming

Mental Health Professions Licensing Board

2020 Carey Ave., Suite 201

Cheyenne, WY 82002

http://plboards.state.wy.us/mentalhealth/index.asp

CERTIFICATION ORGANIZATIONS

American Academy of Orthotists and Prosthetists

526 King St., Suite 201

Alexandria, VA 22314

oandp.org

American Association of State Social Work Boards

400 S. Ridge Pkwy., Suite B

Culpepper, VA 22701

aasswb.org

Contact this organization for a list of regulatory agencies or for a
comparison of state regulations.

American Board of Examiners in Clinical Social Work

Shetland Park

27 Congress St.

Salem, MA 01970

abecsw.org

American Board of Professional Psychology

300 Drayton St., 3rd Floor

Savannah, GA 31401

abpp.org

American Board of Rehabilitation Psychology

2100 E. Broadway, Suite 313

Columbia, MO 65201-6082

apa.org/divisions/div22/ABRP.html

American Dietetic Association
120 S. Riverside Plaza, Suite 2000
Chicago, IL 60606-6995
eatright.org

American Horticultural Therapy Association
201 E. Main St., Suite 1405
Lexington, KY 40507-2004
ahta.org

American Medical Association
515 N. State St.
Chicago, IL 60610
ama-assn.org

American Music Therapy Association, Inc.
8455 Colesville Rd., Suite 1000
Silver Spring, MD 20910
musictherapy.org

American Occupational Therapy Certification Board
4720 Montgomery Ln.
P.O. Box 31220
Bethesda, MD 20824-1220
aota.org

American Physical Therapy Association
1111 N. Fairfax St.
Alexandria, VA 22314-1488
apta.org

American Psychological Association
750 First St. NE, Suite 100
Washington, DC 20002
apa.org

American Speech-Language-Hearing Certification
10801 Rockville Pike
Rockville, MD 20852
asha.org

Art Therapy Credentials Board, Inc.
3 Terrace Way, Suite B
Greensboro, NC 27403
atcb.org

Association of State and Provincial Psychology Boards
P.O. Box 241245
Montgomery, AL 36124-1245
asppb.org

Center for Credentialing and Education, Inc. (CCE)
3 Terrace Way
Greensboro, NC 27403
cce-global.org

Commission on Rehabilitation Counselor Education
300 N. Martingale Rd., Suite 460
Schaumburg, IL 60173
core-rehab.org

Council for Accreditation of Counseling and Related Educational
    Programs
1001 N. Fairfax St., Suite 510
Alexandria, VA 22314
cacrep.org

Council for Higher Education Accreditation
One Dupont Circle NW, Suite 510
Washington, DC 20036-1135
chea.org

Council on Rehabilitation Education
300 N. Martingale Rd., Suite 460
Schaumburg, IL 60173
core-rehab.org

National Board for Certified Counselors
3 Terrace Way
Greensboro, NC 27403
nbcc.org

National Commission on Orthotic and Prosthetic Education
330 John Carlyle St., Suite 200
Alexandria, VA 22314
ncope.org

National Council for Therapeutic Recreation Certification
7 Elmwood Dr.
New City, NY 10956
nctrc.org

APPENDIX

A

U.S. PROFESSIONAL ORGANIZATIONS

American Art Therapy Association, Inc.
5999 Stevenson Ave.
Alexandria, VA 22304
arttherapy.org

American Counseling Association (ACA)
5999 Stevenson Ave.
Alexandria, VA 22304
counseling.org

Divisions of ACA

American College Counseling Association (ACCA)
collegecounseling.org

American Mental Health Counselors Association (AMHCA)
amhca.org

American Rehabilitation Counseling Association (ARCA)
arcaweb.org

American School Counselor Association (ASCA)
schoolcounselor.org

Association for Assessment in Counseling and Education (AACE)
theaaceonline.com

Association for Adult Development and Aging (AADA)
aadaweb.org

Association for Creativity in Counseling (ACC)
aca-acc.org

Association for Counselor Education and Supervision (ACES)
acesonline.net

Association for Counselors and Educators in Government (ACEG)
dantes.doded.mil/dantes_web/organizations/aceg/index.htm

Association for Gay, Lesbian and Bisexual Issues in Counseling
  (AGLBIC)
aglbic.org

Association for Multicultural Counseling and Development (AMCD)
amcdaca.org/amcd/default.cfm

Association for Specialists in Group Work (ASGW)
asgw.org

Association for Spiritual, Ethical, and Religious Values in Counseling
  (ASERVIC)
aservic.org

Counseling Association for Humanistic Education and Development
  (C-AHEAD)
c-ahead.com

Counselors for Social Justice (CSJ)
http://counselorsforsocialjustice.com

International Association of Addictions and Offender Counselors
   (IAAOC)
iaaoc.org

International Association of Marriage and Family Counselors (IAMFC)
iamfc.com

National Career Development Association (NCDA)
http://ncda.org

National Employment Counseling Association (NECA)
employmentcounseling.org/neca.html

American Dance Therapy Association
2000 Century Plaza, Suite 108
10632 Little Patuxent Pkwy.
Columbia, MD 21044
adta.org

American Federation of State, County, and Municipal Employees
1625 L St. NW
Washington, DC 20036
afscme.org

American Geriatrics Society
Empire State Bldg.
350 Fifth Ave., Suite 801
New York, NY 10118
americangeriatrics.org

American Horticultural Therapy Association
201 E. Main St., Suite 1405
Lexington, KY 40507-2004
ahta.org

American Music Therapy Association, Inc.
8455 Colesville Rd., Suite 1000
Silver Spring, MD 20910
musictherapy.org

American Occupational Therapy Association
4720 Montgomery Ln.
P.O. Box 31220
Bethesda, MD 20824-1220
aota.org

American Occupational Therapy Foundation
4720 Montgomery Ln.
P.O. Box 31220
Bethesda, MD 20824-1220
aota.org/featured/area2/index.asp
This website is a source of scholarship information.

American Physical Therapy Association, Inc.
1111 North Fairfax St.
Alexandria, VA 22314-1488
apta.org

American Psychiatric Association
1000 Wilson Blvd., Suite 1825
Arlington, VA 22209-3901
psych.org

American Psychological Association (APA)
750 First St. NE, Suite 100
Washington, DC 20002
apa.org

Divisions of APA

Addictions

Adult Development and Aging

American Psychology-Law Society

American Society for the Advancement of Pharmacotherapy

Applied Experimental and Engineering Psychology

Behavior Analysis

Behavioral Neuroscience and Comparative Psychology

Clinical Neuropsychology

Developmental Psychology

Educational Psychology

Evaluation, Measurement, and Statistics

Exercise and Sport Psychology

Experimental Psychology

Family Psychology

Group Psychology and Group Psychotherapy

Health Psychology

Humanistic Psychology

Intellectual and Developmental Disabilities

International Psychology

Media Psychology

Population and Environmental Psychology

Psychoanalysis

Psychologists in Independent Practice

Psychologists in Public Service

Psychology of Religion

Psychopharmacology and Substance Abuse

Psychotherapy

Rehabilitation Psychology

School Psychology

Society for Child and Family Policy and Practice

Society for Community Research and Action: Division of Community
  Psychology

Society for Consumer Psychology

Society for General Psychology

Society for Industrial and Organizational Psychology

Society for Military Psychology

Society for Personality and Social Psychology

Society for the History of Psychology

Society for the Psychological Study of Ethnic Minority Issues

Society for the Psychological Study of Lesbian, Gay, and Bisexual Issues

Society for the Psychological Study of Men and Masculinity

Society for the Psychological Study of Social Issues (SPSSI)

Society for the Psychology of Aesthetics, Creativity and the Arts

Society for the Psychology of Women

Society for the Study of Peace, Conflict, and Violence: Peace Psychology
  Division

Society for the Teaching of Psychology

Society for Theoretical and Philosophical Psychology

Society of Clinical Child and Adolescent Psychology

Society of Clinical Psychology

Society of Consulting Psychology

Society of Counseling Psychology

Society of Pediatric Psychology

Society of Psychological Hypnosis

State, Provincial, and Territorial Psychological Association Affairs

Trauma Psychology

American Therapeutic Recreation Association
1414 Prince St., Suite 204
Alexandria, VA 22314
atra-tr.org

Association for Career and Technical Education
1410 King St.
Alexandria, VA 22314
acteonline.org

Association for Play Therapy, Inc.
2060 N. Winery Ave., Suite 102
Fresno, CA 93703
a4pt.org

Council on Rehabilitation Education
300 N. Martingale Rd., Suite 460
Schaumburg, IL 60173
core-rehab.org

Council on Social Work Education
1725 Duke St., Suite 500
Alexandria, VA 22314
cswe.org
This organization publishes the *Directory of Accredited B.S.W. and M.S.W. Programs.*

Hebrew Union College
Jewish Institute of Religion
One W. Fourth St.
New York, NY 10012
huc.edu

Jewish Theological Seminary of America
3080 Broadway
New York, NY 10027
jtsa.edu

National Association of Colleges and Employers
62 Highland Ave.
Bethlehem, PA 18017-9085
naceweb.org

National Association of School Psychologists
4340 East West Hwy., Suite 402
Bethesda, MD 20814
naspweb.org

National Association of Social Workers (NASW)
750 First St. NE, Suite 700
Washington, DC 20002-4241
naswdc.org
Information about NASW's specialty practice sections is available at
naswdc.org/sections/default.asp

Aging

Alcohol, Tobacco and Other Drugs

Children, Adolescents and Young Adults

Child Welfare

Health

Mental Health

Private Practice

School Social Work

Social and Economic Justice and Peace

National Clearinghouse on Alcoholism and Drug Abuse Information
P.O. Box 2345
Rockville, MD 20852
http://ncadi.samhsa.gov

National Coalition for Church Vocations
5420 S. Cornell Ave. #105
Chicago, IL 60615-5604
nccv-vocations.org

National Council on Disability
1331 F St. NW, Suite 805
Washington, DC 20004
ncd.gov

National Council on Rehabilitation Education
2012 W. Norwood Dr.
Carbondale, IL 62901
rehabeducators.org

National Institute on Drug Abuse
6001 Executive Blvd.
Bethesda, MD 20892-9561
nida.nih.gov

National Recreation and Park Association
22377 Belmont Ridge Rd.
Ashburn, VA 20148
nrpa.org

National Rehabilitation Association
633 S. Washington St.
Alexandria, VA 22314
nationalrehab.org

National Rehabilitation Counseling Association
P.O. Box 4480
Manassas, VA 20108
nrca-net.org

People-Plant Council
Department of Horticulture
Virginia Polytechnic Institute and State University
Blacksburg, VA 24061
hort.vt.edu/human/PPC.html

A P P E N D I X

B

CANADIAN PROFESSIONAL ORGANIZATIONS

Association of Social Workers of Northern Canada
Box 2963
Yellowknife, NT X1A 2R2
socialworknorth.com

Canadian Art Therapy Association
Box 538
Birtle, MB R0M 0C0
catainfo.ca

Canadian Association for Music Therapists
Wilfrid Laurier University
Waterloo, ON N2L 3C5
musictherapy.ca

Canadian Association for Pastoral Practice and Education
7960 St. Margaret's Bay Rd.
Ingramport, NS B3Z 3Z7
cappe.org

Canadian Association for Prosthetics and Orthotics
605-294 Portage Ave.
Winnipeg, MB R3C 0B9
pando.ca

Canadian Association of College and University Student Services
4 Cataraqui St., Suite 310
Kingston, ON K7K 1Z7
cacuss.ca/en/index.lasso

Canadian Association of Occupational Therapists
CTTC Bldg., Suite 3400
1125 Colonel By Dr.
Ottawa, ON K1S 5R1
caot.ca

Canadian Association of Rehabilitation Professionals Inc.
302–201 Consumers Rd.
Toronto, ON M2J 4G8
carpnational.org

Canadian Association of School Psychologists
10660 Trepassey Dr.
Richmond, BC V7E 4K7
cpa.ca/casp/index.html

Canadian Association of School Social Workers and Attendance
   Counsellors
76 Bluewater Crescent
Winnipeg, MB R2J 2P8
http://casswac.ca/default.asp

Canadian Association of Schools of Social Work
1398 ch. Star Top Rd.
Ottawa, ON K13 4V7
cassw-acess.ca

Canadian Association of Social Workers
383 Parkdale Ave., Suite 402
Ottawa, ON K1Y 4R4
casw-acts.ca

CASW Member Organizations

Alberta College of Social Workers
#550, 10707 100 Ave. NW
Edmonton, AB T5J 3M1
acsw.ab.ca

British Columbia Association of Social Workers
Suite 402, 1755 W. Broadway
Vancouver, BC V6J 4S5
bcasw.org

Manitoba Association of Social Workers
Unit 4, 2015 Portage Ave.
Winnipeg, MB R3J 0K3
maswmirsw.ca

New Brunswick Association of Social Workers
P.O. Box 1533, Postal Station A
Fredericton, NS E3B 5G2
nbasw-atsnb.ca

Newfoundland and Labrador Association of Social Workers
P.O. Box 5244, East End Post Office
St. John's, NF (T-N) AIC 5W1
nlasw.ca

Nova Scotia Association of Social Workers
1891 Brunswick St., Suite 106
Halifax, NS B3J 21G8
nsasw.org

Ontario Association of Social Workers
410 Jarvis St.
Toronto, ON M4Y 2G6
oasw.org

Prince Edward Island Association of Social Workers
81 Prince St.
Charlottetown, PE C1A 4R3

Saskatchewan Association of Social Workers
2110 Lorne St.
Regina, SK S4P 2M5
sasw.ca

Canadian Association of Speech-Language Pathologists and Audiologists
920 - 1 Nicholas St.
Ottawa, ON K1N 7B7
caslpa.ca

Canadian Career Development Foundation
119 Ross Ave., Suite 202
Ottawa, ON K1Y 0N6
ccdf.ca/ccdf2

Canadian Consortium for Collaborative Mental Health Care
10 George St., 3rd Floor
Hamilton, ON L8P 1C8
shared-care.ca

Canadian Counseling Association
16 Concourse Gate, Suite 600
Ottawa, ON K2E 7S8
ccacc.ca

Canadian Employee Assistance Program Association
1031 Portage Ave.
Winnipeg, MB R3G 0R8
ceapa.ca/index.htm

Canadian Horticultural Therapy Association
70 Westmount Rd.
Guelph, ON N1H 5H8
chta.ca

Canadian Mental Health Association
180 Dundas St. W., Suite 2301
Toronto, ON M5G 1Z8
cmha.ca/bins/index.asp

Canadian Network of Substance Abuse and Allied Professionals
(CNSAAP)
75 Albert St., Suite 300
Ottawa, ON K1P 5E7
cnsaap.ca/cnsaap

Canadian Nurses Association
50 Driveway
Ottawa, ON K2P 1E2
cna-nurses.ca

Canadian Physical Medicine and Rehabilitation Services Associations
Suite 312, 902 - 11th Ave. SW
Calgary, AB T2R 0E7
http://canadianwellness.com/physical/physical_associations.asp

Canadian Physiotherapy Association (CPA)
2345 Yonge St., Suite 410
Toronto, ON M4P 2E5
physiotherapy.ca

Canadian Professional Counsellors Association
#203, 3306 - 32nd Ave.
Vernon, BC V1T 2M6
cpca-rpc.ca

Canadian Psychiatric Association (CPA)
141 Laurier Ave. W., Suite 701
Ottawa, ON K1P 5J3
http://ww1.cpa-apc.org:8080/index.asp

Canadian Psychological Association
141 Laurier Ave. W., Suite 702
Ottawa, ON K1P 5J3
cpa.ca/home

Provincial Chapters of CPA

Psychologists' Association of Alberta
520 Metropolitan Place
10303 Jasper Ave.
Edmonton, AB T5J 3N6
psychologistsassociation.ab.ca

British Columbia Psychological Association
Suite 202, 1755 W. Broadway
Vancouver, BC V6J 4S5
psychologists.bc.ca

Manitoba Psychological Society Inc.
FW208-CSB, 820 Sherbrook St.
Winnipeg, MB R3A 1R9
mps.mb.ca

Association of Psychologists of Nova Scotia
1657 Barrington St., Suite 417
Halifax, NS B3J 2A1
apns.ca

Ontario Psychological Association
730 Yonge St., Suite 221
Toronto, ON M4Y 2B7
psych.on.ca

Ordre des Psychologues du Québec
1100 Ave. Beaumont, Bureau 510
Mont-Royal, QU H3P 3E5
ordrepsy.qc.ca/opqv2/fra/index.asp

Canadian Therapeutic Recreation Association
8038 Fairmount Drive SE
Calgary, AB T2H 0Y1
canadian-tr.org

Dietitians of Canada
480 University Ave., Suite 604
Toronto, ON M5G 1V2
dietitians.ca

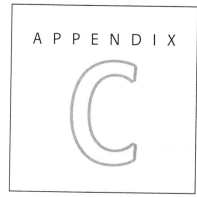

APPENDIX

C

WEBSITES
OF INTEREST

American Academy of Counseling Psychology
aacop.net

American Association for Geriatric Psychiatry
aagpgpa.org

American Association for Marriage and Family Therapy
aamft.org

American Association for Psychology and the Performing Arts
http://srb123.tripod.com/AAPPA.html

American Association of Pastoral Counselors
aapc.org

American Association of State Social Work Boards
aasswb.org

American Board of Examiners in Clinical Social Work
abecsw.org

American Board of Professional Psychology
abpp.org

American Medical Association
ama-assn.org

American Psychiatric Nurses Association
apna.org

American Psychoanalytic Association
http://apsa.org

Asian American Psychological Association
aapaonline.org/index.shtml

Association for Death Education and Counseling
adec.org

Association for Psychological Science
psychologicalscience.org

Association for the Advancement of Psychology
aapnet.org

Association of Black Psychologists
abpsi.org

Clinical Social Work Federation
cswf.org

Institute of Gerontology, Wayne State University
iog.wayne.edu

International Association of Applied Psychology
iaapsy.org

International Association of Cognitive Psychotherapy
cognitivetherapyassociation.org

International Federation of Social Workers
ifsw.org

Manitoba Institute of Registered Social Workers
maswmirsw.ca

National Institute on Alcohol Abuse and Alcoholism
niaaa.nih.gov

Society for Computers in Psychology
http://home.scip.ws

Society for Industrial and Organizational Psychology
siop.org

Society for Personality and Social Psychology
spsp.org

Society for Police and Criminal Psychology
http://psychweb.cisat.jmu.edu/spcp

United States Psychiatric Rehabilitation Association
uspra.org

World Council for Psychotherapy
psychotherapie.at/wcp

World Health Organization
who.ch

APPENDIX

D

U.S. UNIVERSITIES AND COLLEGES

Following is a sampling of the schools offering graduate and undergraduate programs in social and rehabilitation services. Go to these websites for information about individual universities and colleges.

UNIVERSITIES AND COLLEGES WITH PROGRAMS IN BOTH SOCIAL WORK AND REHABILITATION COUNSELING

Auburn University (AL)
auburn.edu

California State University at Fresno
csufresno.edu

California State University at Sacramento
csus.edu

California State University at San Bernardino
csusb.edu

Florida State University
fsu.edu

Jackson State University (MS)
jsums.edu

Louisiana State University
lsu.edu

Michigan State University
msu.edu

Minnesota State University at Mankato
mnsu.edu

New York University
nyu.edu

Ohio State University
osu.edu

Portland State University (OR)
pdx.edu

San Diego State University (CA)
sdsu.edu

St. Cloud State University (MN)
stcloudstate.edu

Syracuse University (NY)
syr.edu

University of Arkansas at Little Rock
ualr.edu

University of Georgia
uga.edu

University of Hawaii at Manoa
http://manoa.hawaii.edu

University of Illinois at Urbana-Champaign
uiuc.edu

University of Kentucky
uky.edu

University of Maryland at Baltimore County
umbc.edu

University of Missouri
missouri.edu

University of North Carolina at Chapel Hill
unc.edu

University of Tennessee at Knoxville
utk.edu

Utah State University
usu.edu

Virginia Commonwealth University
vcu.edu

Wayne State University (MI)
wayne.edu

West Virginia University
wvu.edu

UNIVERSITIES AND COLLEGES WITH SOCIAL WORK PROGRAMS

Adelphi University (NY)
adelphi.edu

Andrews University (MI)
andrews.edu

Arizona State University
asu.edu

Ashland University (OH)
ashland.edu

Austin Peay State University (TN)
apsu.edu

Ball State University (IN)
bsu.edu

Barry University (FL)
barry.edu

Baylor University (TX)
baylor.edu

Bloomsburg University (PA)
bloomu.edu

Boston College
bc.edu

Boston University
bu.edu

Brigham Young University (UT)
byu.edu

Bryn Mawr College (PA)
brynmawr.edu

Central Michigan University
cmich.edu

Clark Atlanta University (GA)
cau.edu

Columbia University (NY)
columbia.edu

Delta State University (MS)
deltastate.edu

Eastern Washington University (WA)
ewu.edu

Ferrum College (VA)
ferrum.edu/indexjava.htm

Florida International University
fiu.edu/choice.html

Gallaudet University (DC)
gallaudet.edu

Hood College (MD)
hood.edu

Hope College (MI)
hope.edu

Hunter College (NY)
hunter.cuny.edu

Idaho State University
isu.edu

Indiana University
indiana.edu

James Madison University (VA)
jmu.edu

Kansas State University
ksu.edu

Kean University (NJ)
kean.edu

Loma Linda University (CA)
llu.edu

Loyola University Chicago
luc.edu

Marian College (WI)
mariancollege.edu

Monmouth University (NJ)
monmouth.edu

Nebraska Wesleyan University
nebrwesleyan.edu

New Mexico State University
nmsu.edu

North Carolina State University
ncsu.edu

Northern Arizona University
nau.edu

Oklahoma Baptist University
okbu.edu

Pacific Lutheran University (WA)
plu.edu

Saginaw Valley State University (MI)
svsu.edu

Shippensburg University (PA)
ship.edu

Temple University (PA)
temple.edu

Texas Woman's University
twu.edu

Trevecca Nazarene University (TN)
trevecca.edu

Tulane University (LA)
tulane.edu

University of Alaska at Anchorage
http://socwork.uaa.alaska.edu

University of Chicago
uchicago.edu

University of Cincinnati
uc.edu

University of Denver
du.edu

University of Minnesota
umn.edu

University of Montana
umt.edu

Walla Walla College (WA)
wwc.edu/nav

Washington University at St. Louis (MO)
wustl.edu

Xavier University (OH)
xu.edu

Yeshiva University (NY)
yu.edu

UNIVERSITIES AND COLLEGES WITH REHABILITATION COUNSELING PROGRAMS

Alabama A&M University
aamu.edu

Arkansas State University
asumh.edu

Assumption College (MA)
assumption.edu

Bowling Green State University (OH)
bgsu.edu

Coppin State College (MD)
coppin.edu

Drake University (IA)
drake.edu

East Central University (OK)
ecok.edu

Edinboro University of Pennsylvania
edinboro.edu

Fort Valley State University (GA)
fvsu.edu

George Washington University (DC)
gwu.edu

Georgia State University
gsu.edu

Hofstra University (NY)
hofstra.edu

Illinois Institute of Technology
iit.edu

Kent State University (OH)
kent.edu

Mississippi State University
msstate.edu

Montana State University at Billings
msubillings.edu

Northeastern University (MA)
northeastern.edu

Pennsylvania State University
psu.edu

San Francisco State University (CA)
sfsu.edu

South Carolina State University
scsu.edu

Springfield College (MA)
spfldcol.edu

Stephen F. Austin State University (TX)
sfasu.edu

University of Arizona
arizona.edu

University of Florida
ufl.edu

University of Idaho
uidaho.edu

University of Iowa
uiowa.edu

University of Massachusetts at Boston
umb.edu

University of Memphis (TN)
memphis.edu

University of Northern Colorado
univnorthco.edu

University of Puerto Rico
upr.clu.edu

University of Scranton (PA)
scranton.edu

University of Southern Maine
usm.maine.edu

University of Texas at Austin
utexas.edu

Western Oregon University
wou.edu

Wright State University (OH)
wright.edu

CANADIAN SCHOOLS OF SOCIAL WORK

Carleton University
carleton.ca/ssw

Dalhousie University
socialwork.dal.ca

First Nations University of Canada
School of Indian Social Work
firstnationsuniversity.ca/depsw

King's University College
University of Western Ontario
uwo.ca/kings

Lakehead University
lakeheadu.ca

Laurentian University/Université Laurentienne
laurentian.ca/social_work

McGill University
mcgill.ca/socialwork

McMaster University
socsci.mcmaster.ca/socwork

Memorial University of Newfoundland
mun.ca

Nicola Valley Institute of Technology
nvit.bc.ca

Renison College
renison.uwaterloo.ca/social-work

Ryerson University
ryerson.ca

St. Thomas University
stu.ca

Thompson Rivers University
tru.ca/psd/social/swhome.htm

Université de Moncton
umoncton.ca

Université de Montréal
fas.umontreal.ca/esersoc

Université de Sherbrooke
usherbrooke.ca

Université d'Ottawa
servicesocial.uottawa.ca

Université du Québec à Chicoutimi
uqac.uquebec.ca

Université du Québec à Montréal
travailsocial.uqam.ca

Université du Québec en Abitibi-Témiscamingue
uqat.ca

Université du Québec en Outaouais
uqo.ca

Université Laval
svs.ulaval.ca

University College of the Fraser Valley
ucfv.ca/swhs

University of British Columbia
swfs.ubc.ca

University of British Columbia Okanagan
http://ubc.ca/okanagan/welcome.html

University of Calgary
http://fsw.ucalgary.ca

University of Manitoba
umanitoba.ca/faculties/social_work

University of Northern British Columbia
unbc.ca/socialwork

University of Regina
uregina.ca

University of Toronto
socialwork.utoronto.ca

University of Victoria
uvic.ca/socw

University of Windsor
uwindsor.ca/faculty/socwk/index.html

Wilfrid Laurier University
wlu.ca/socialwork

York University
atkinson.yorku.ca/sowk

ABOUT
THE AUTHOR

Geraldine O. Garner taught graduate and undergraduate courses in career development in the Rehabilitation Counseling Department at Virginia Commonwealth University (VCU). She also served as an associate dean in VCU's former School of Community and Public Affairs. Today, she is president of STCS, Inc., and works with employers in the health-care field that are concerned about retaining their top talent.

Dr. Garner holds a doctorate in career counseling from Virginia Tech and bachelor's and master's degrees from the College of William and Mary. She is the author of a variety of books, articles, and papers and has received many honors for her work in career counseling and career development.